TRIBE

A Colouring Book
for relaxation and rejuvenation

Cassie Haywood

ISBN: 978-0-9944431-3-7

A CIP record for this book is available from the National Library of Australia

TRIBE

Tribal designs have a deep history established in story telling with a sense of meaning and belonging to many cultures throughout the world. The different patterns radiate courage, strength, passion, and hence reflect the vitality of the people and their landscape. A tribe is about feeling connected, grounded, at peace, understood and at one with each other, mother nature, and the world.

In this book you will find 50 illustrations inspired by Tribal patterns from all over the world. Simply choose an illustration which appeals to you, take a few deep breaths and start colouring. There are no rules to follow, you choose the medium and colours which speak to you. These illustrations open the way for letting go and inner peace, therefore allowing relaxation and rejuvenation to become part of your everyday life.

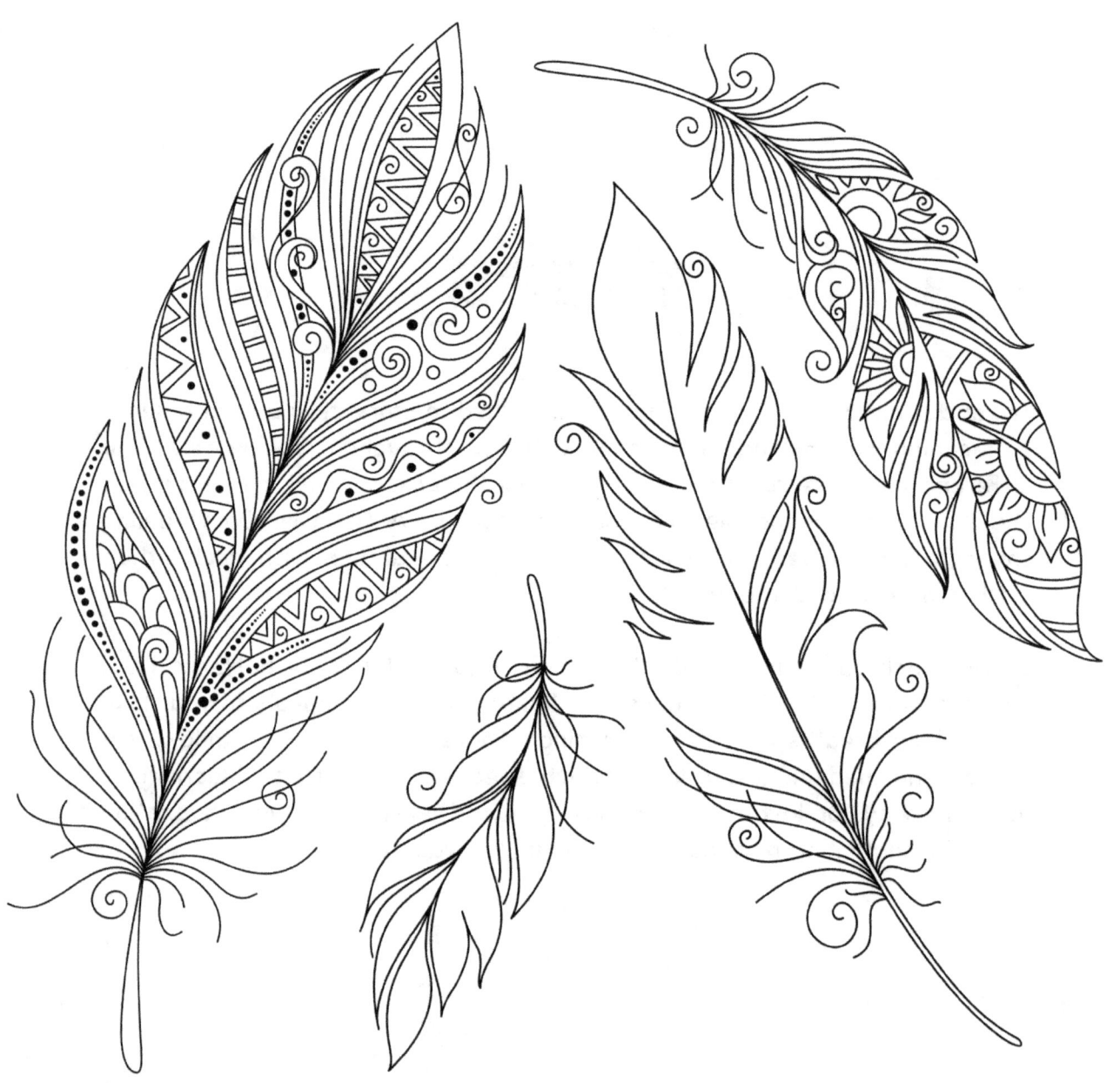

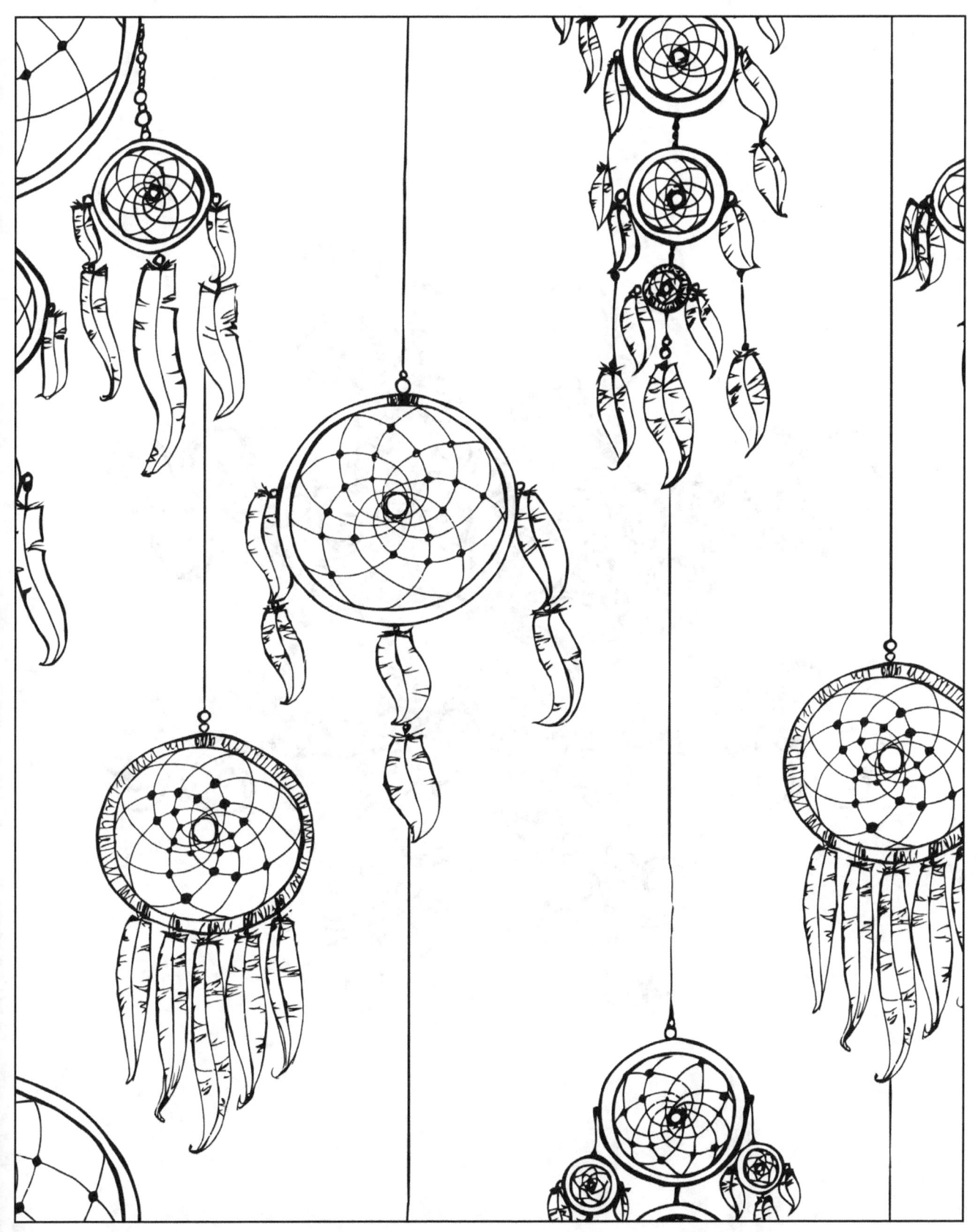

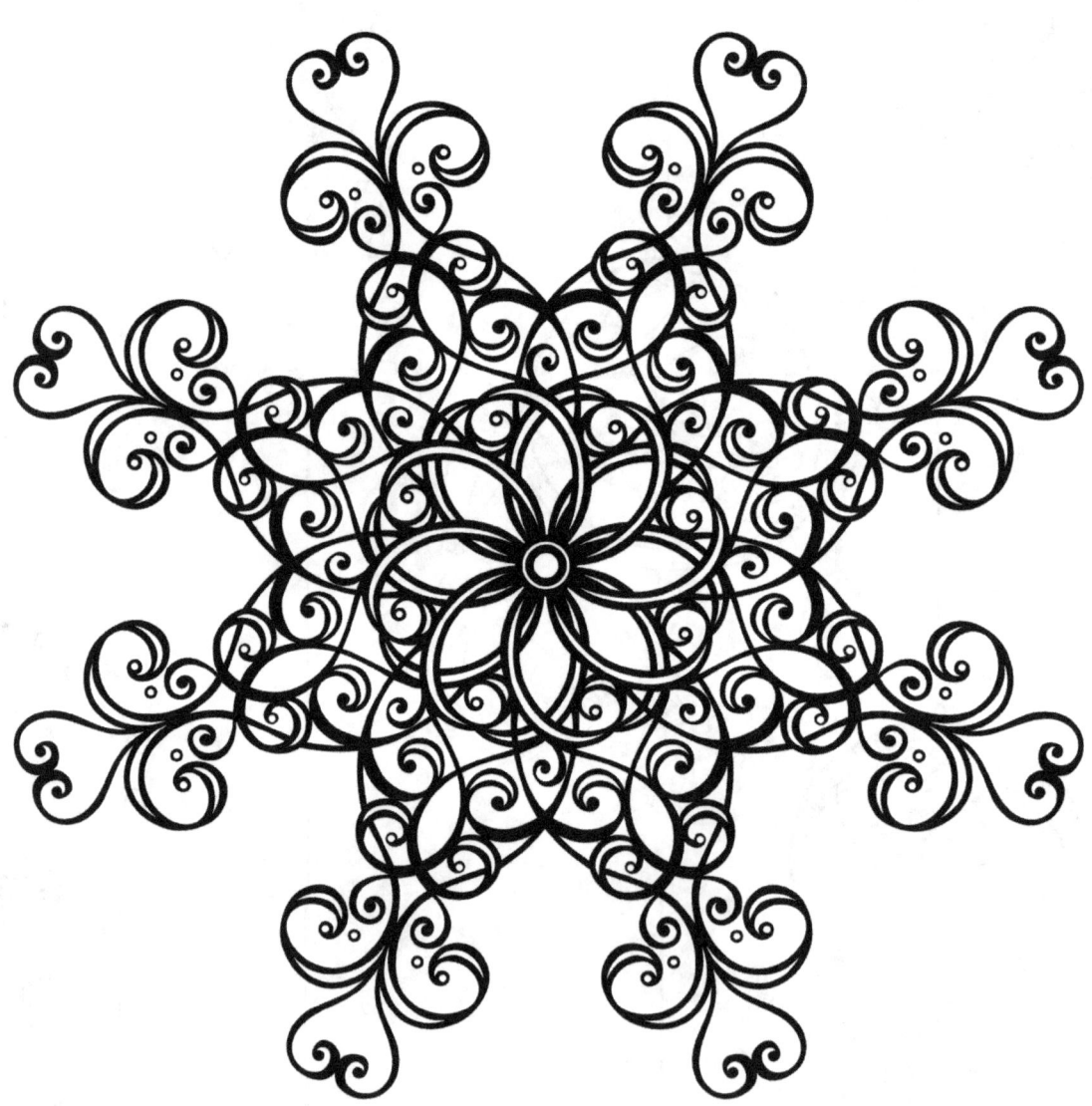

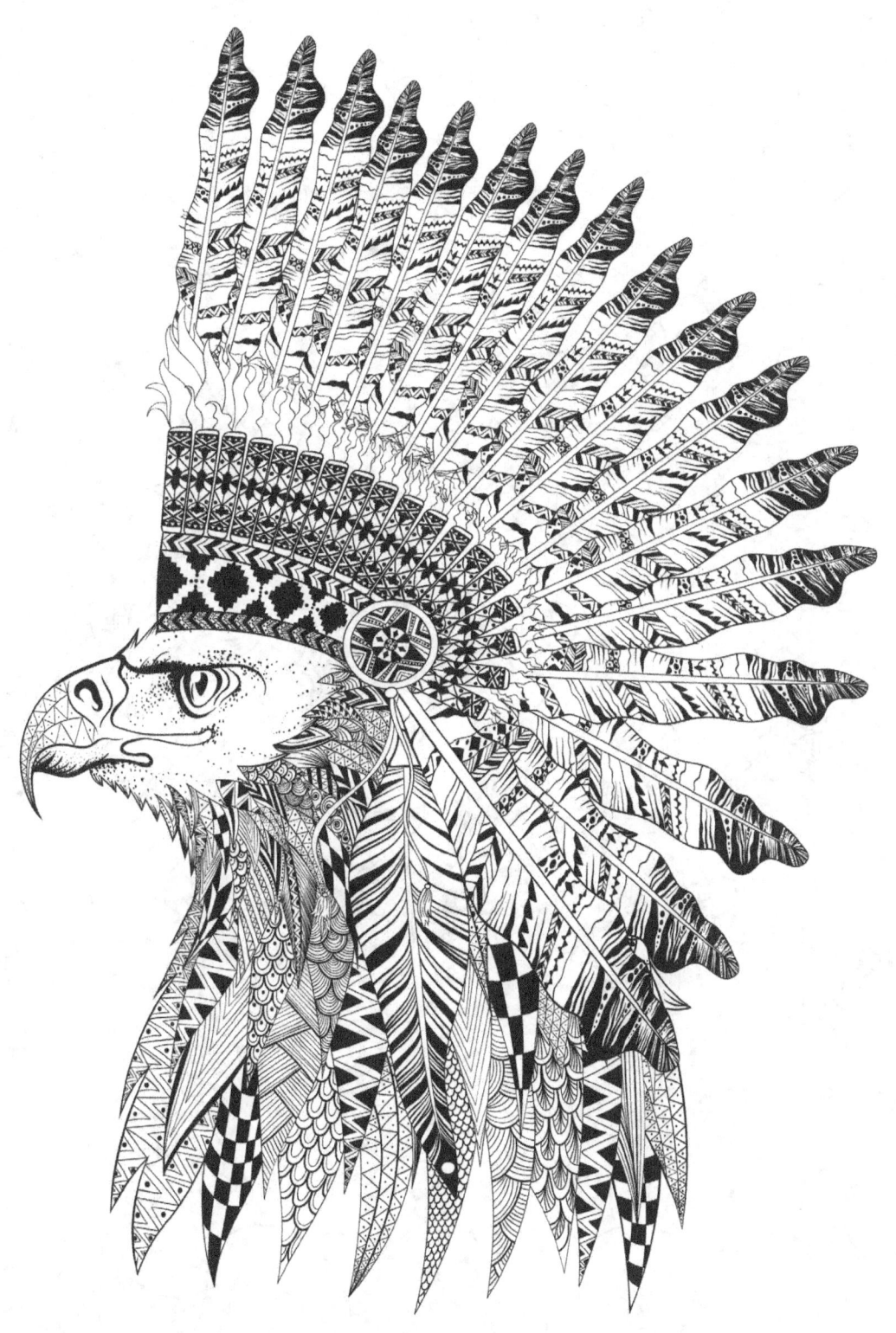

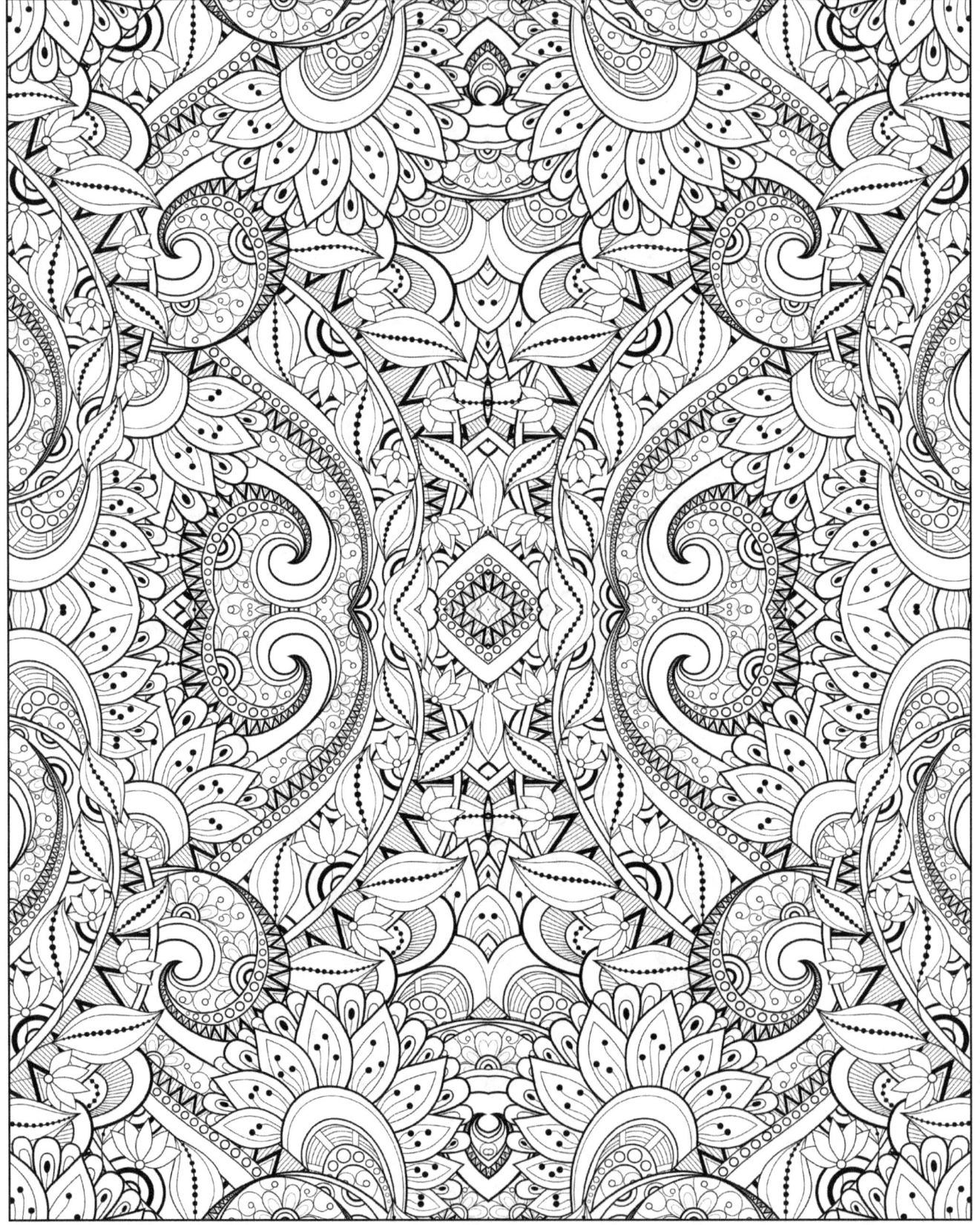

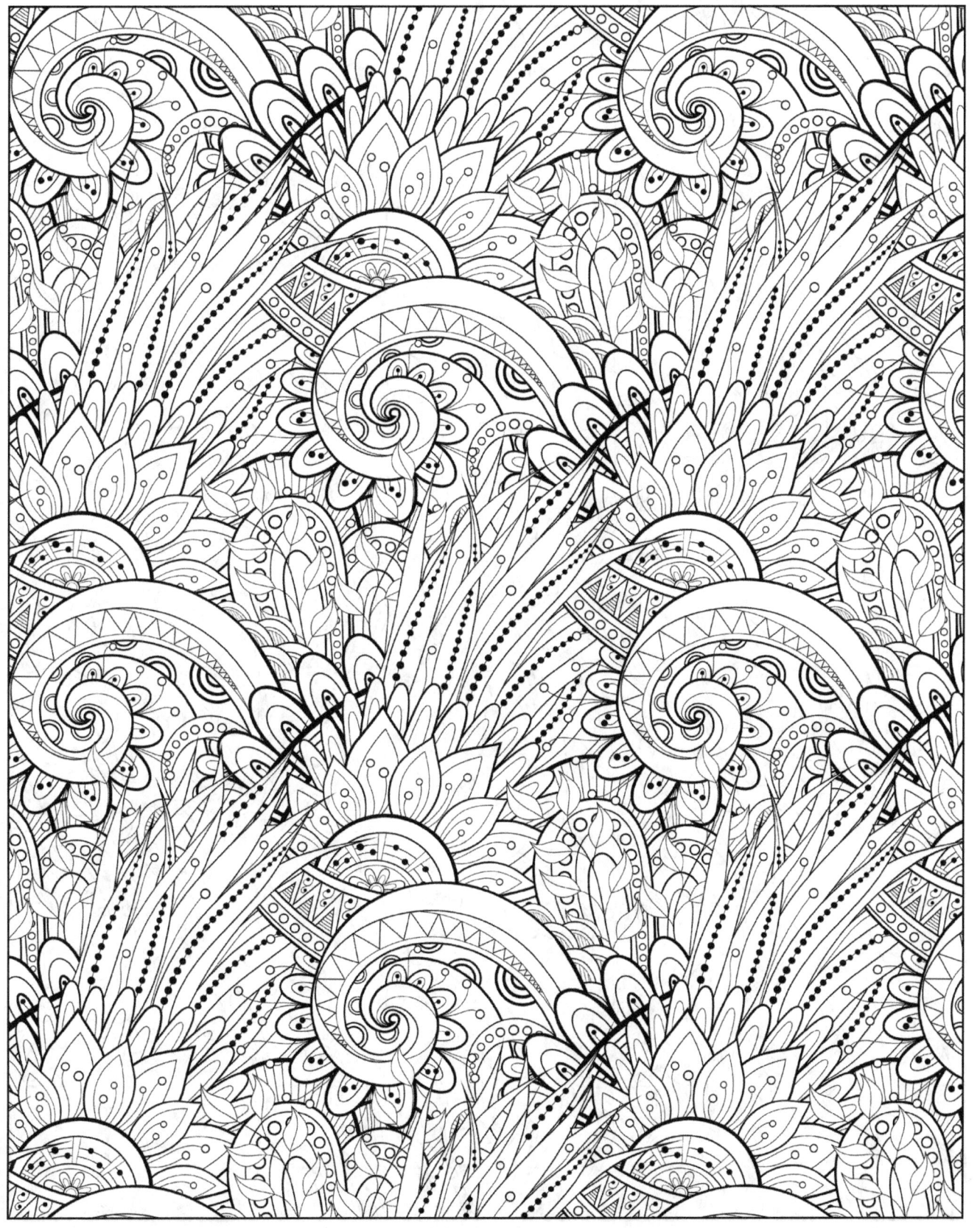

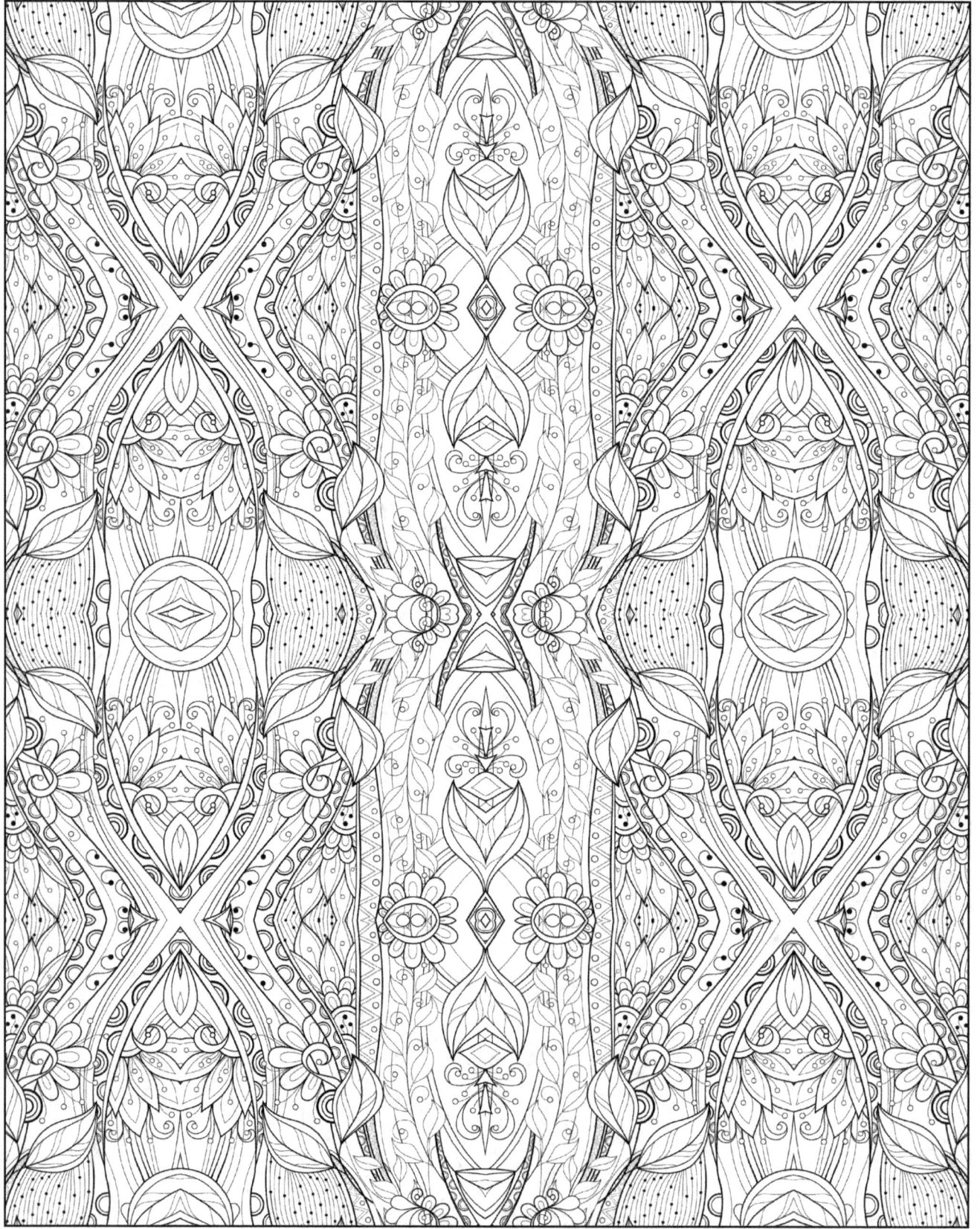

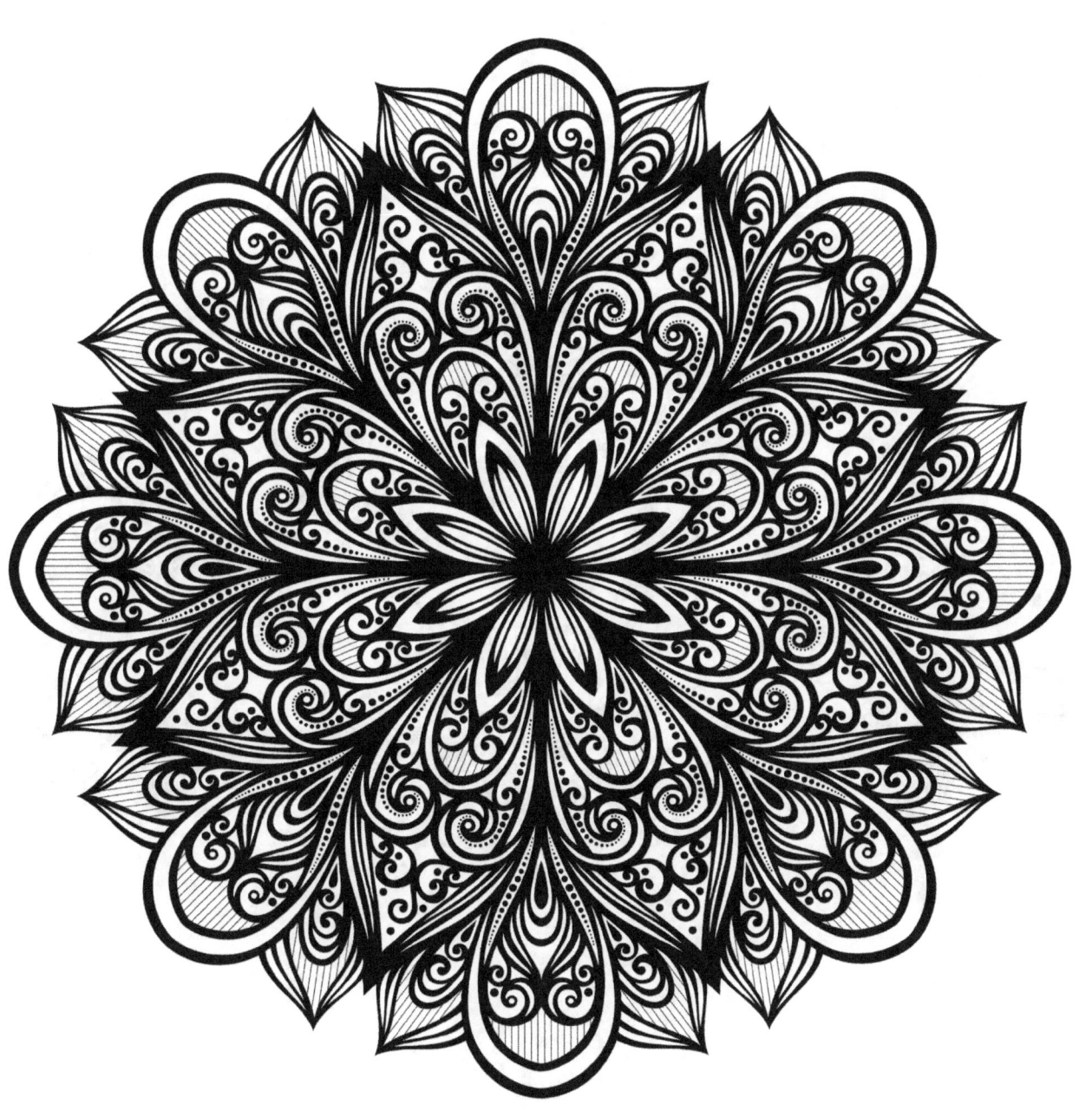

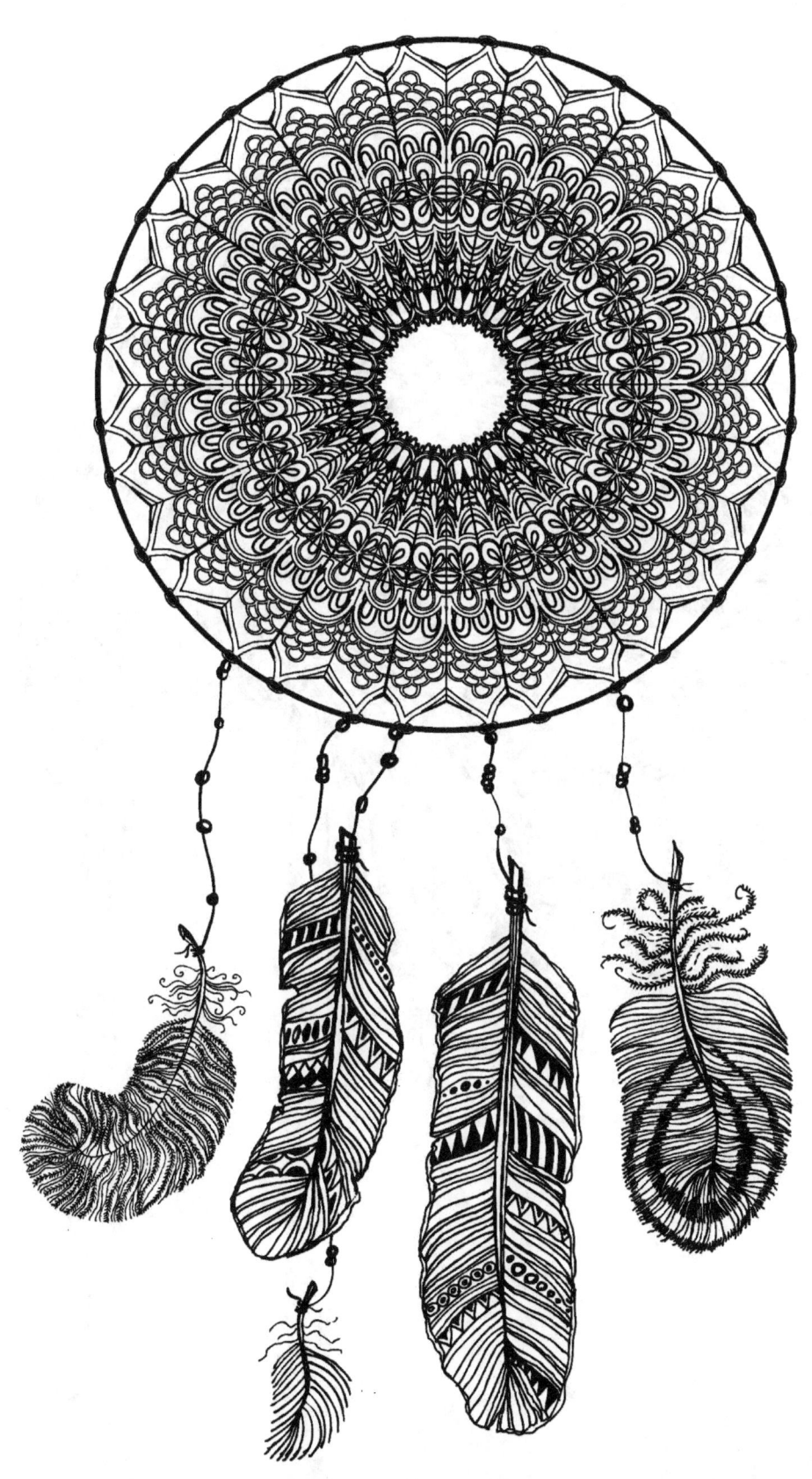

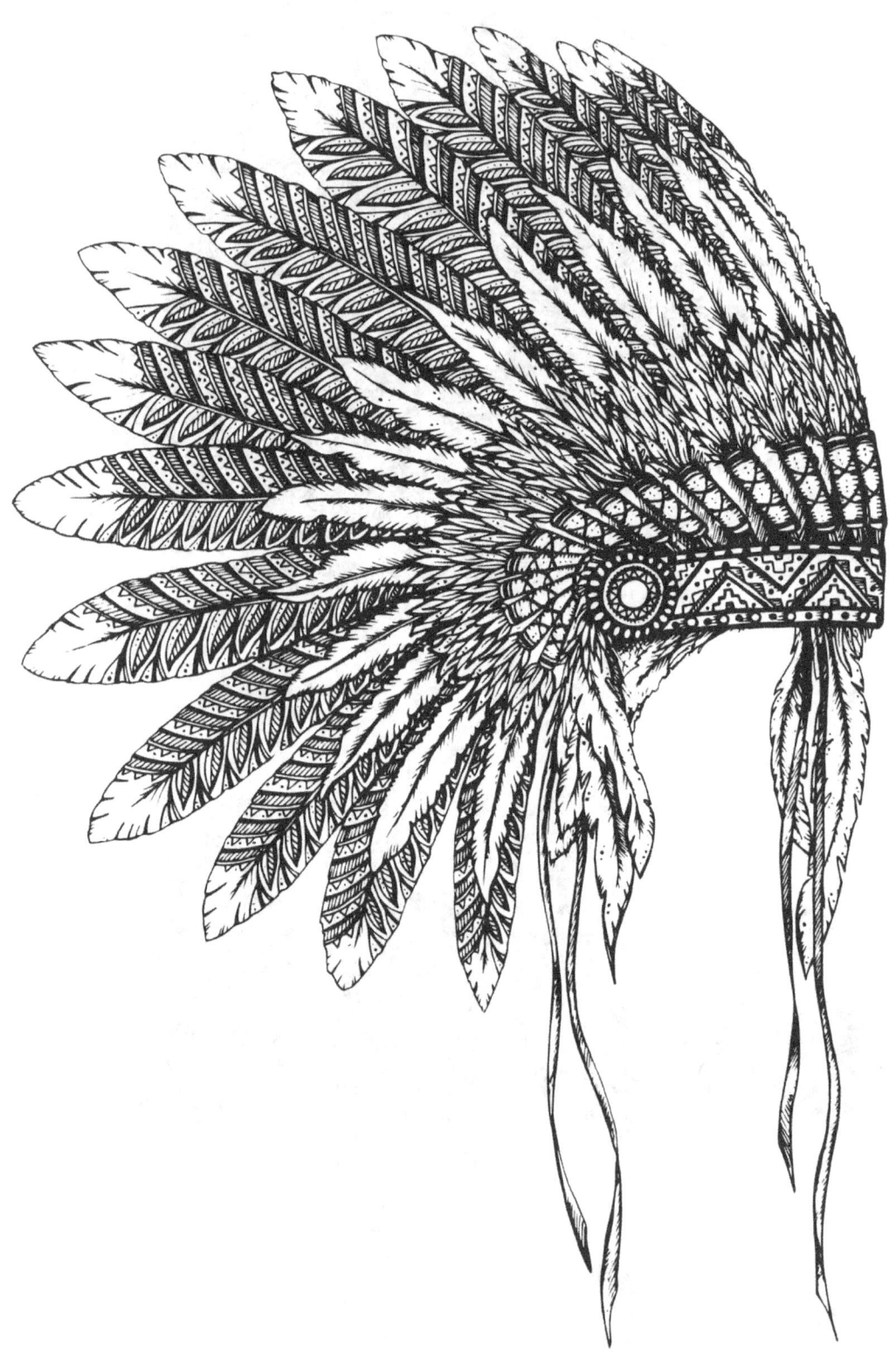

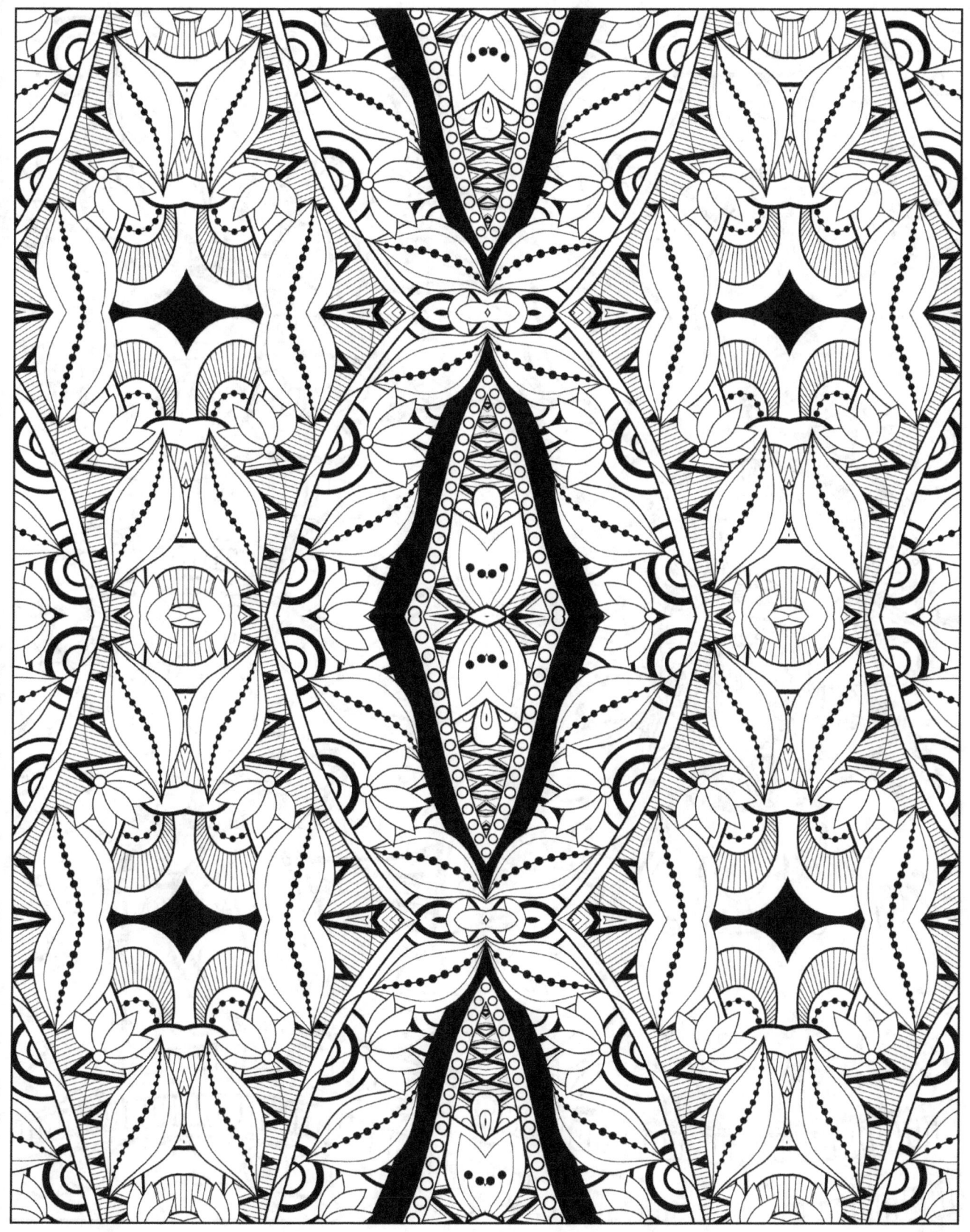

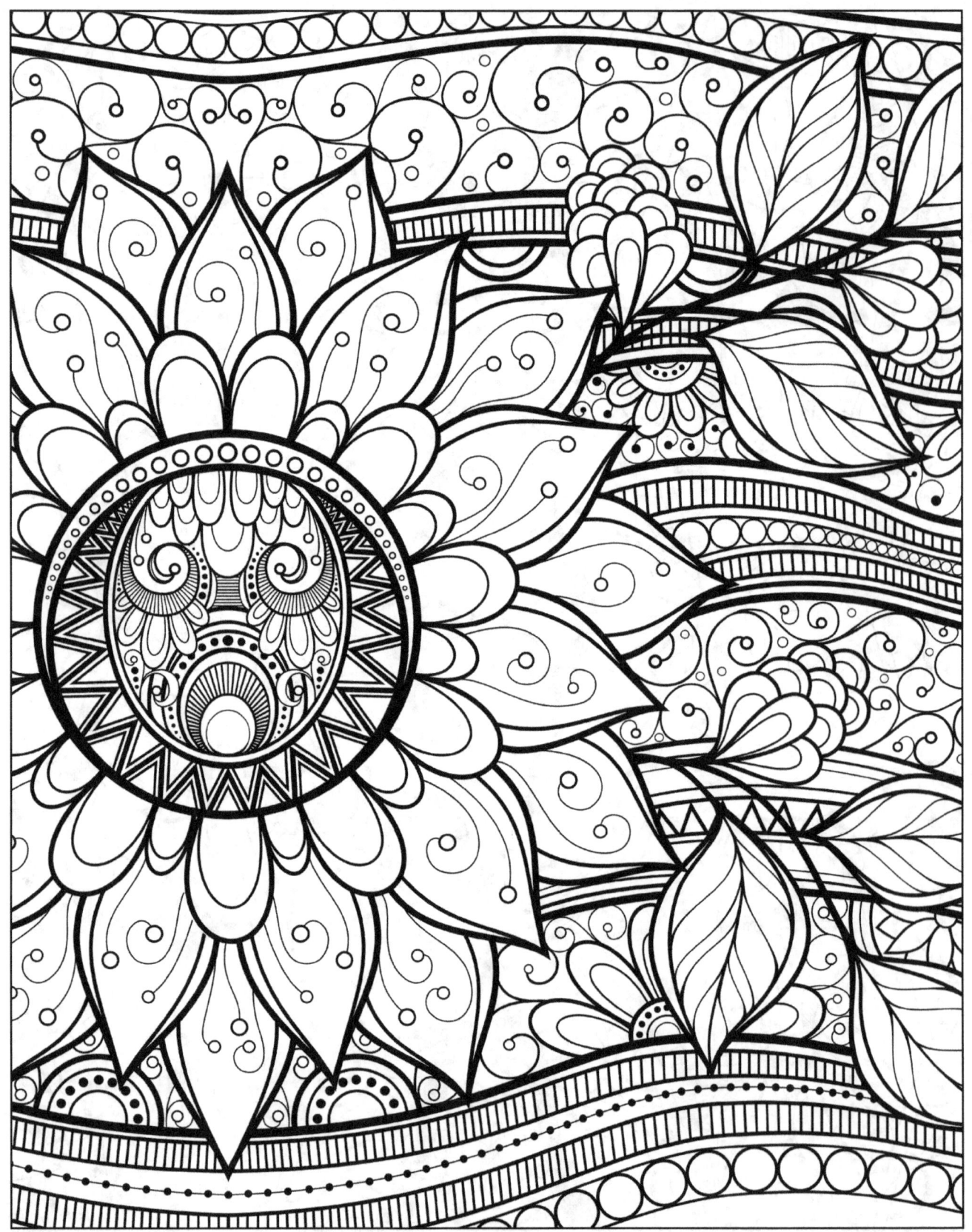

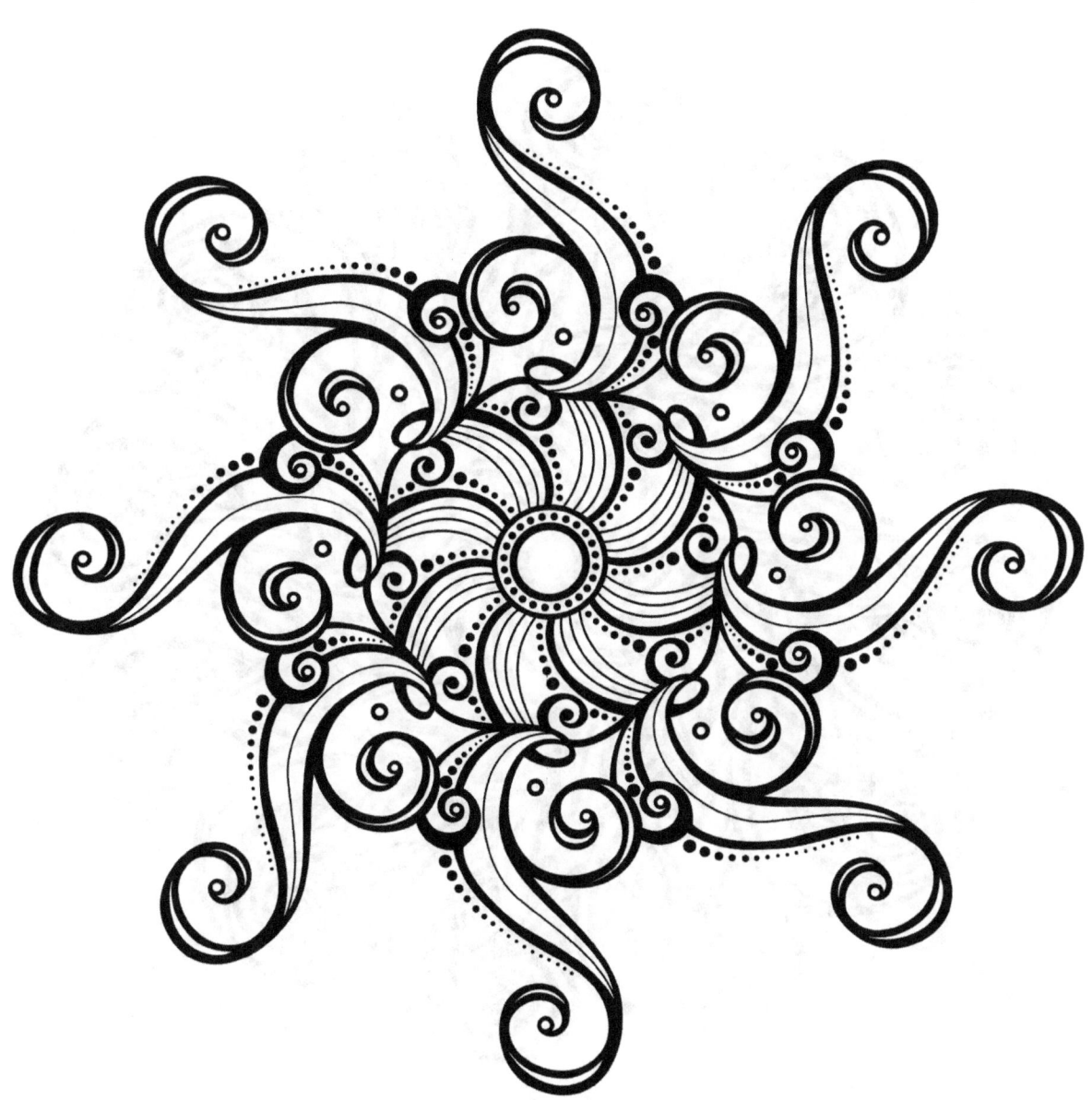

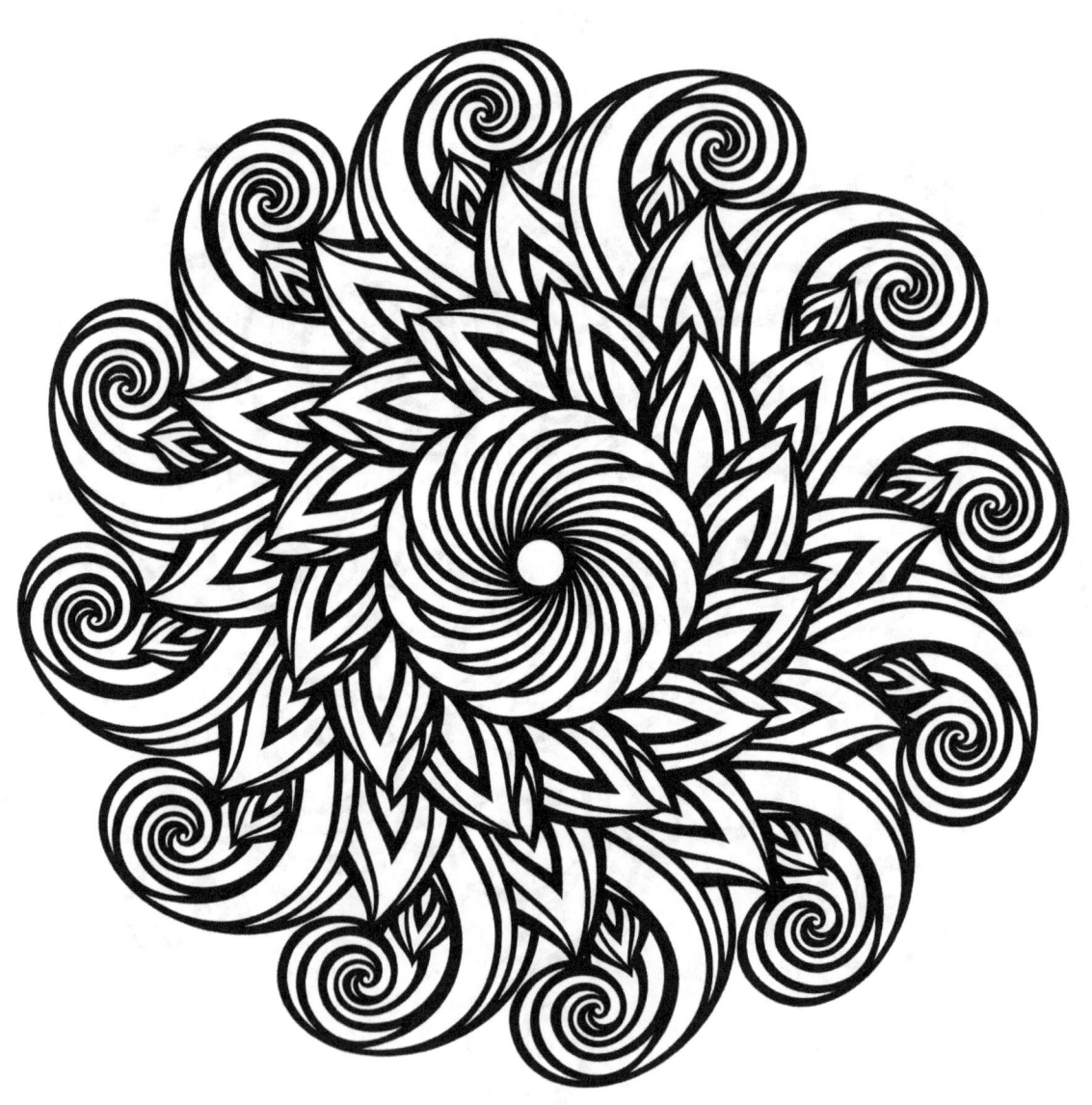

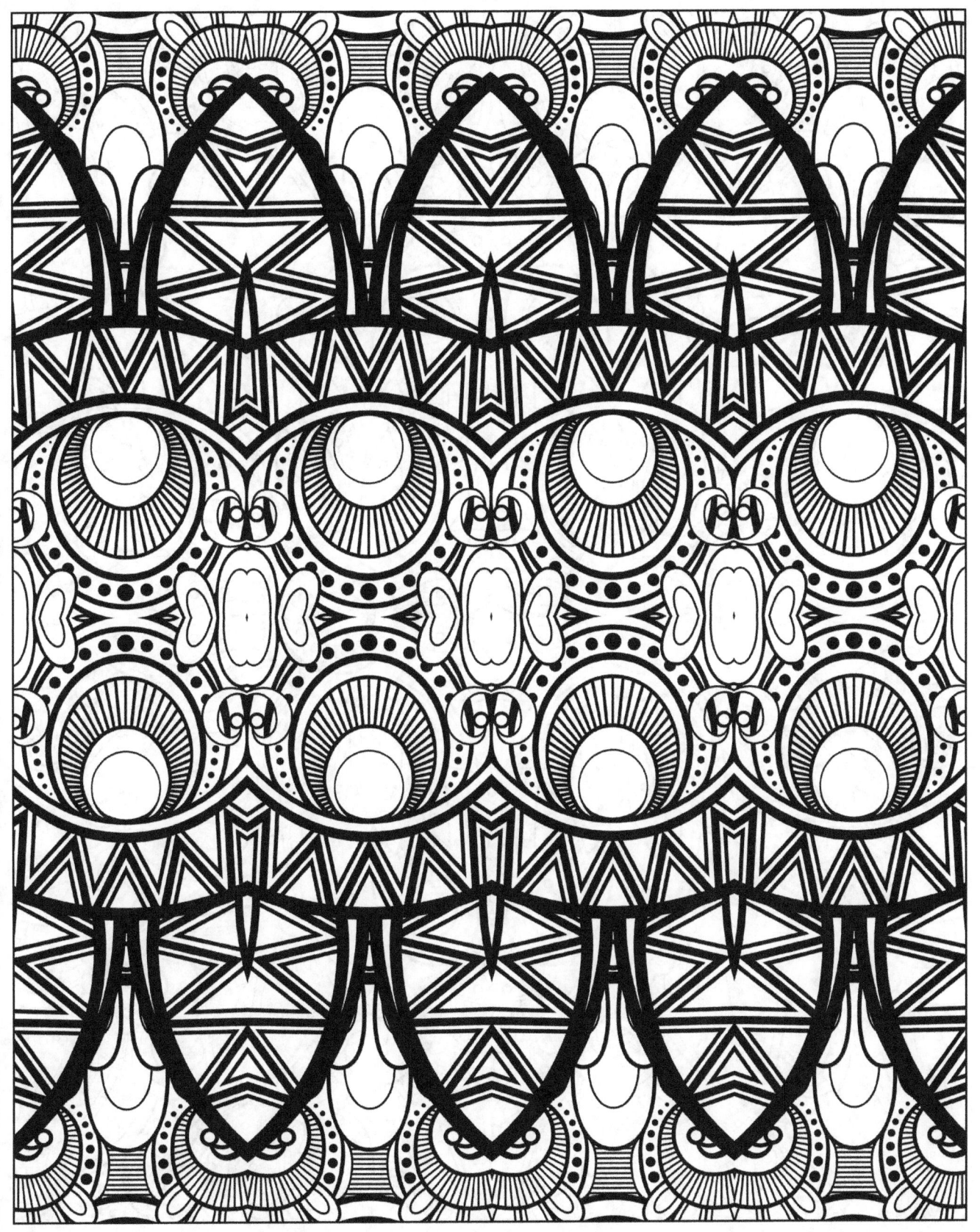

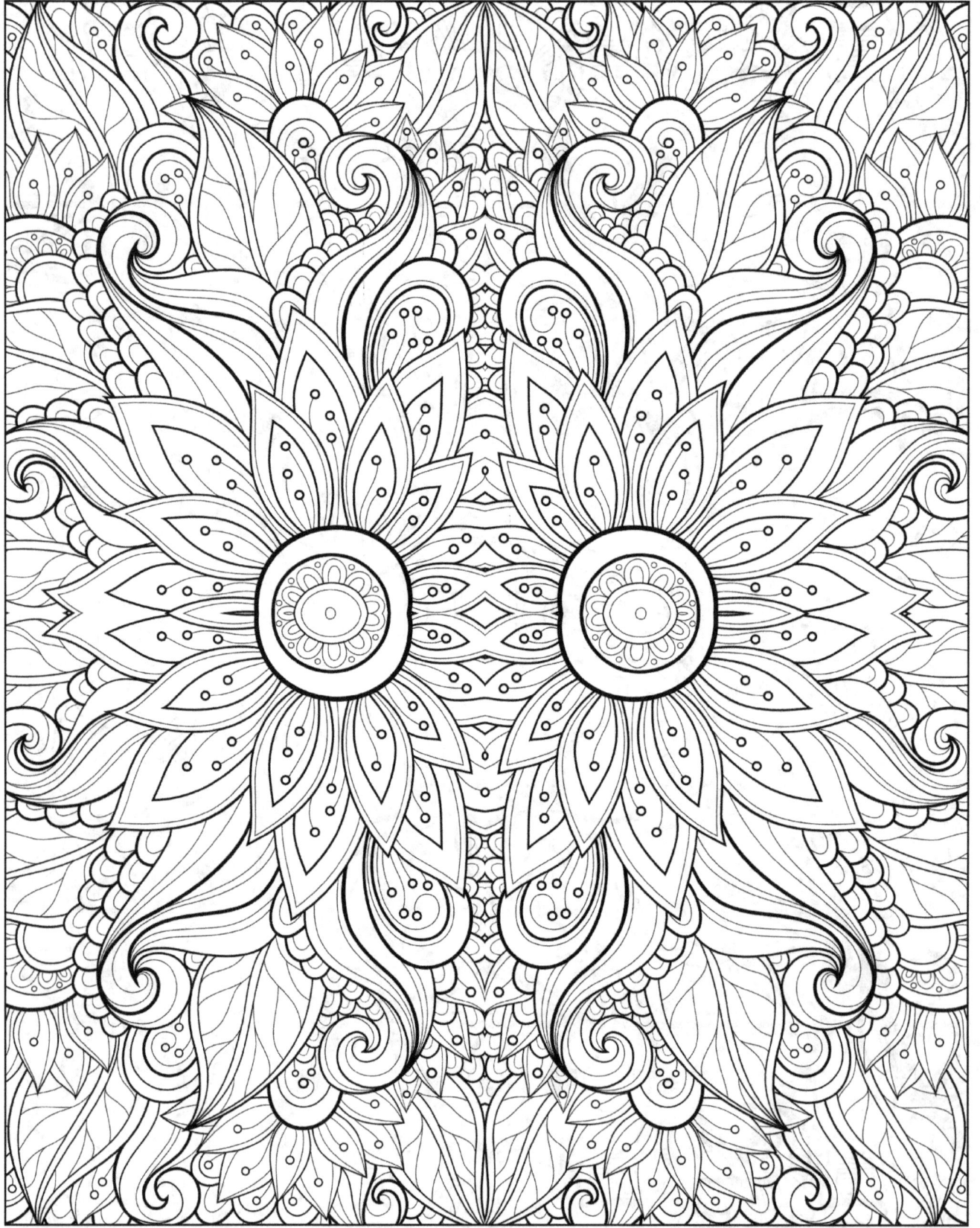

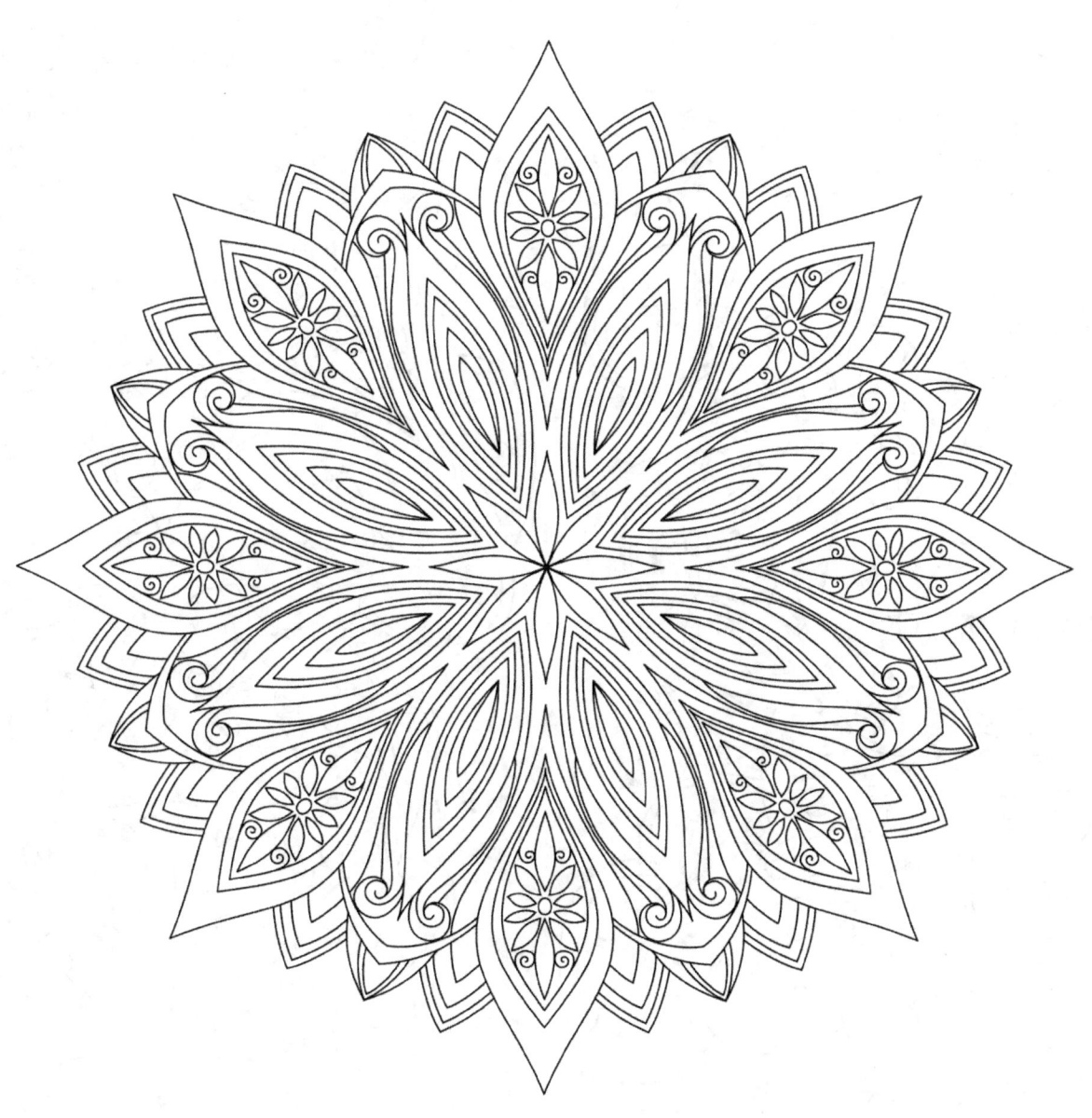

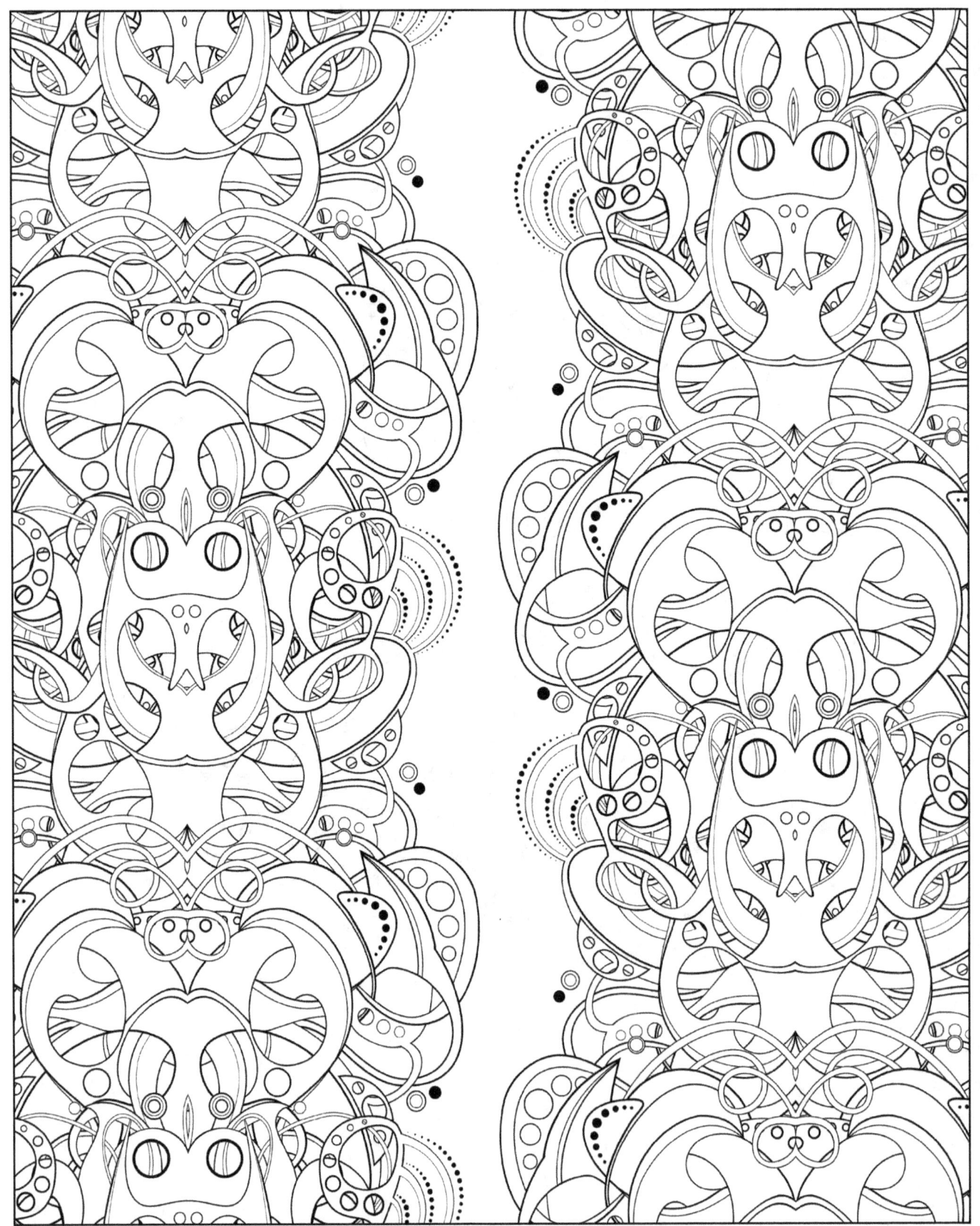

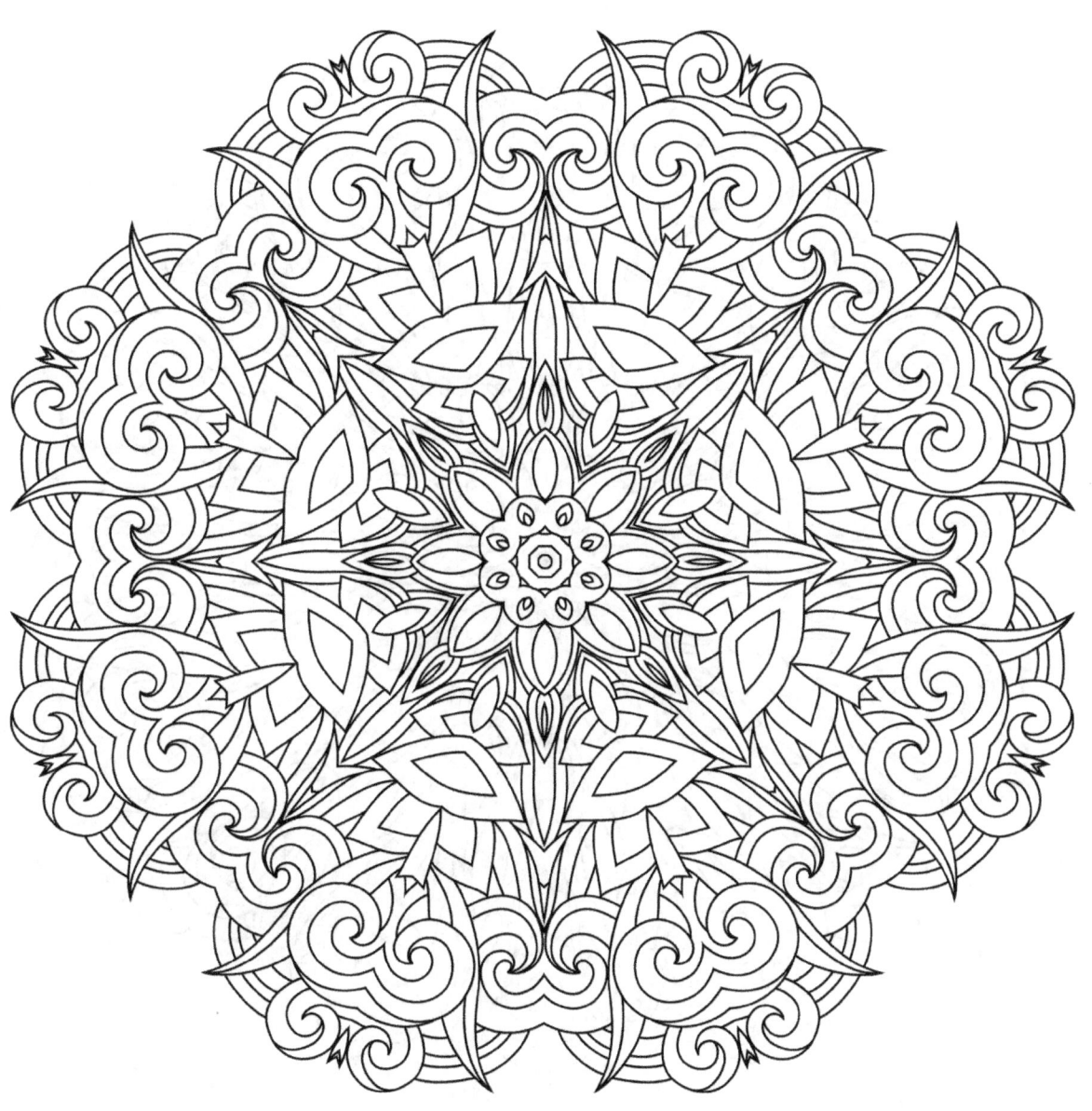

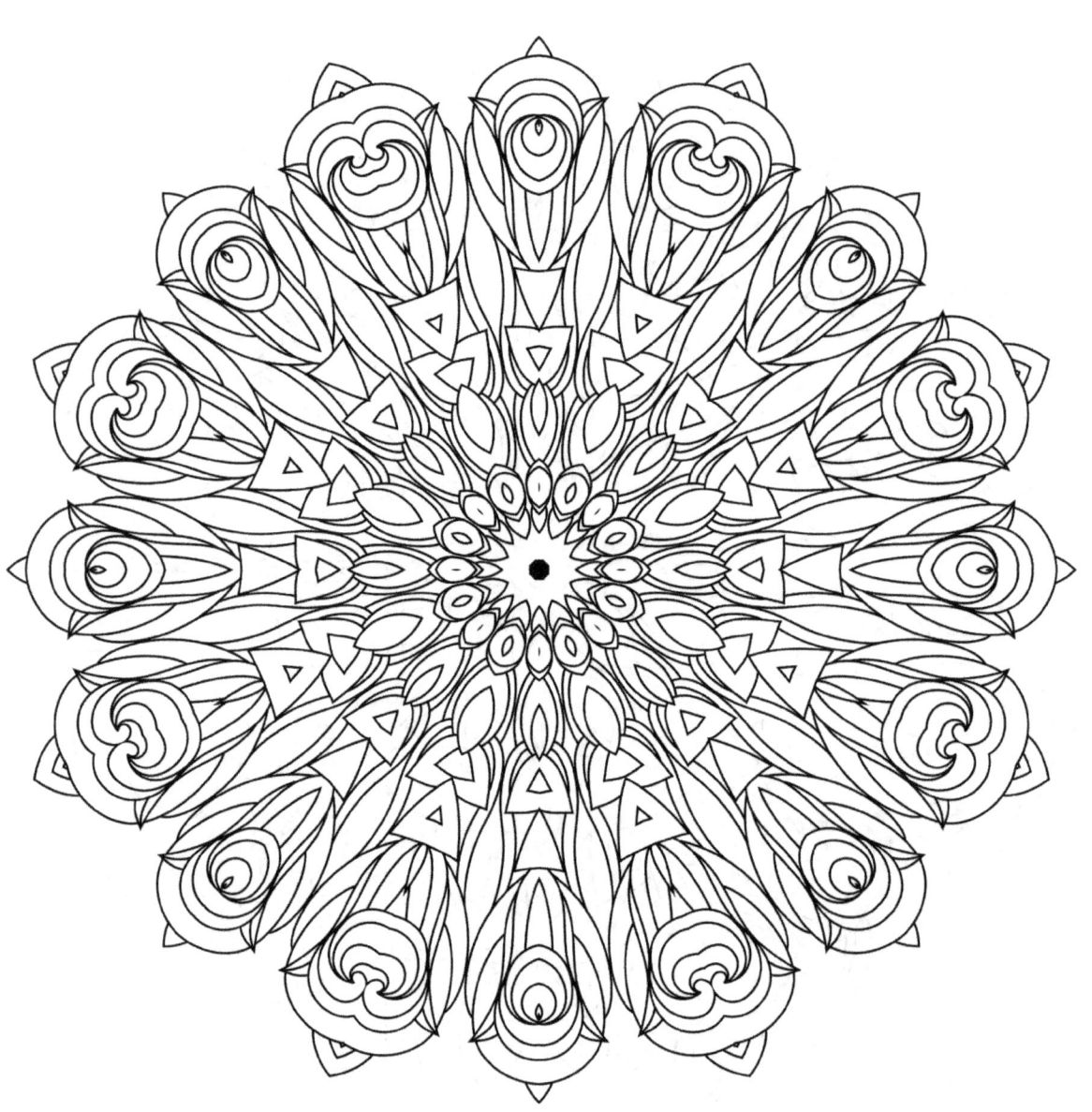

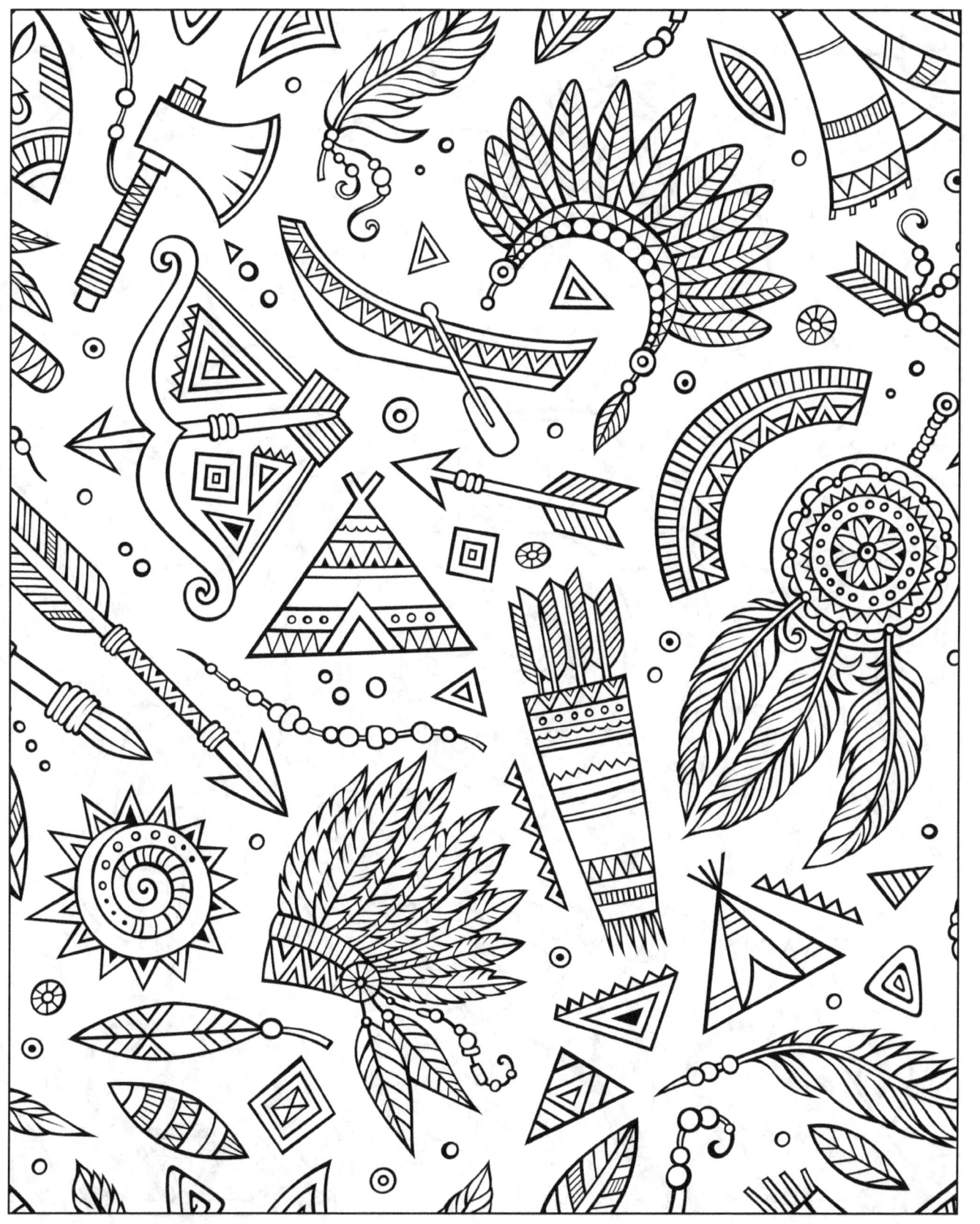

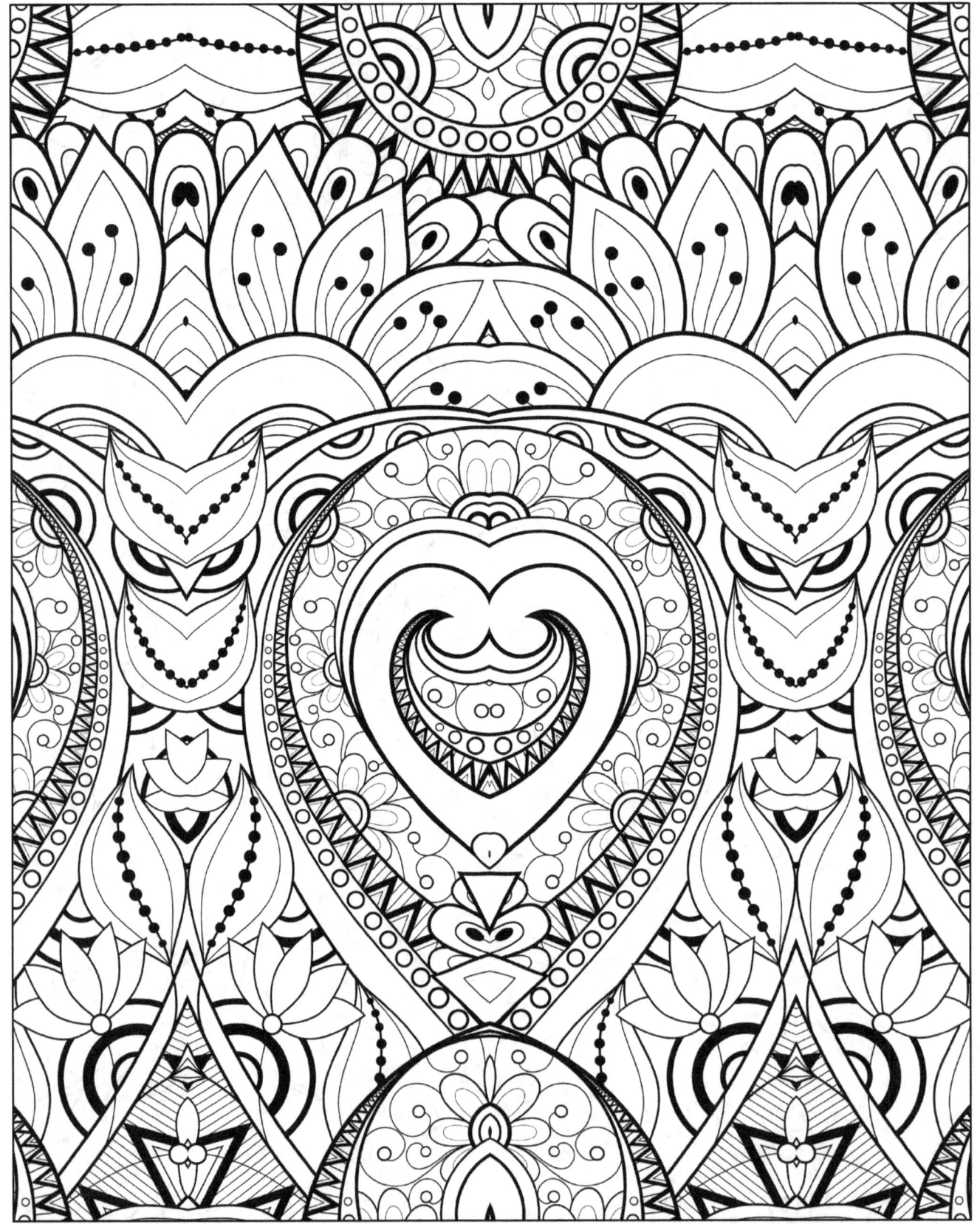

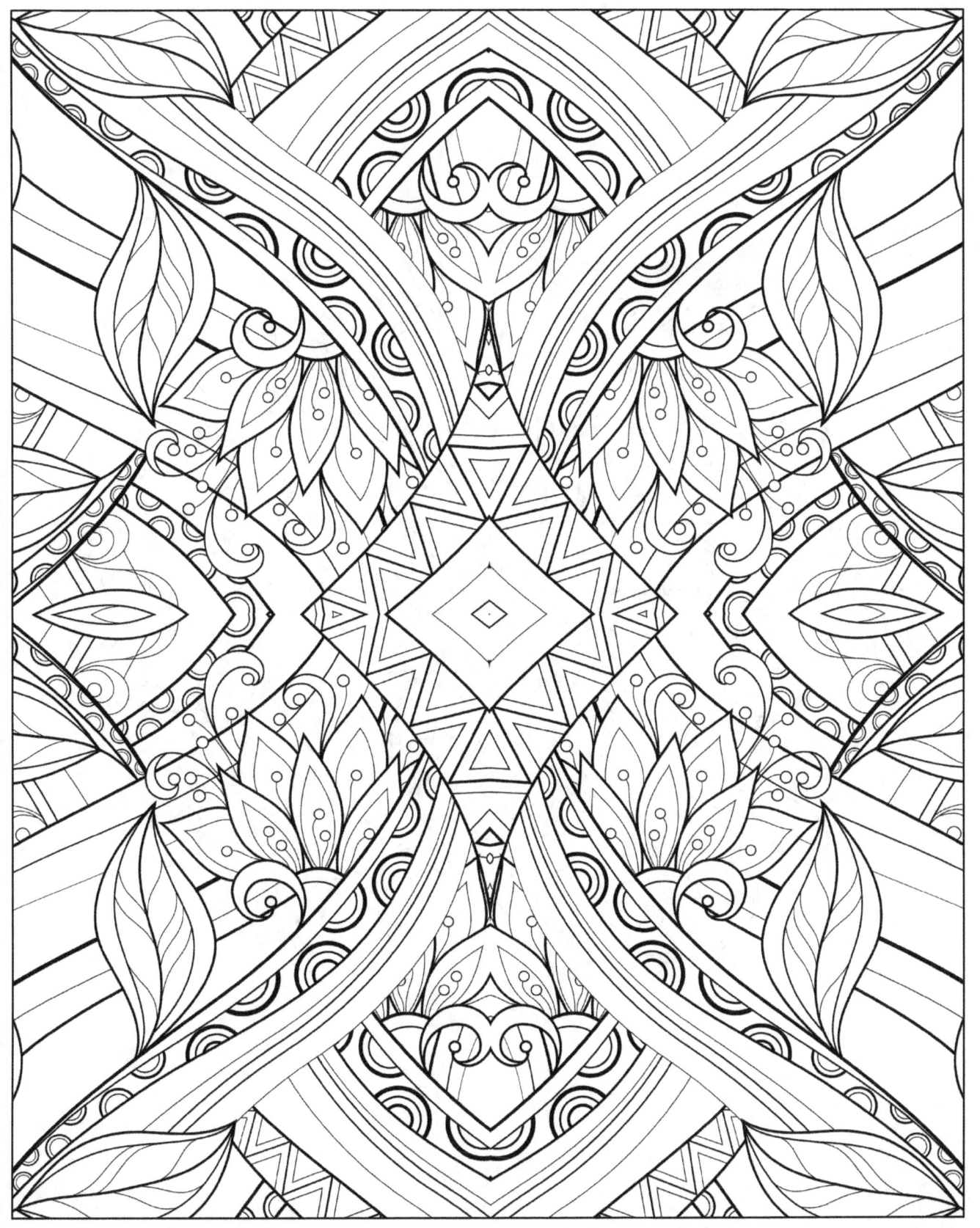

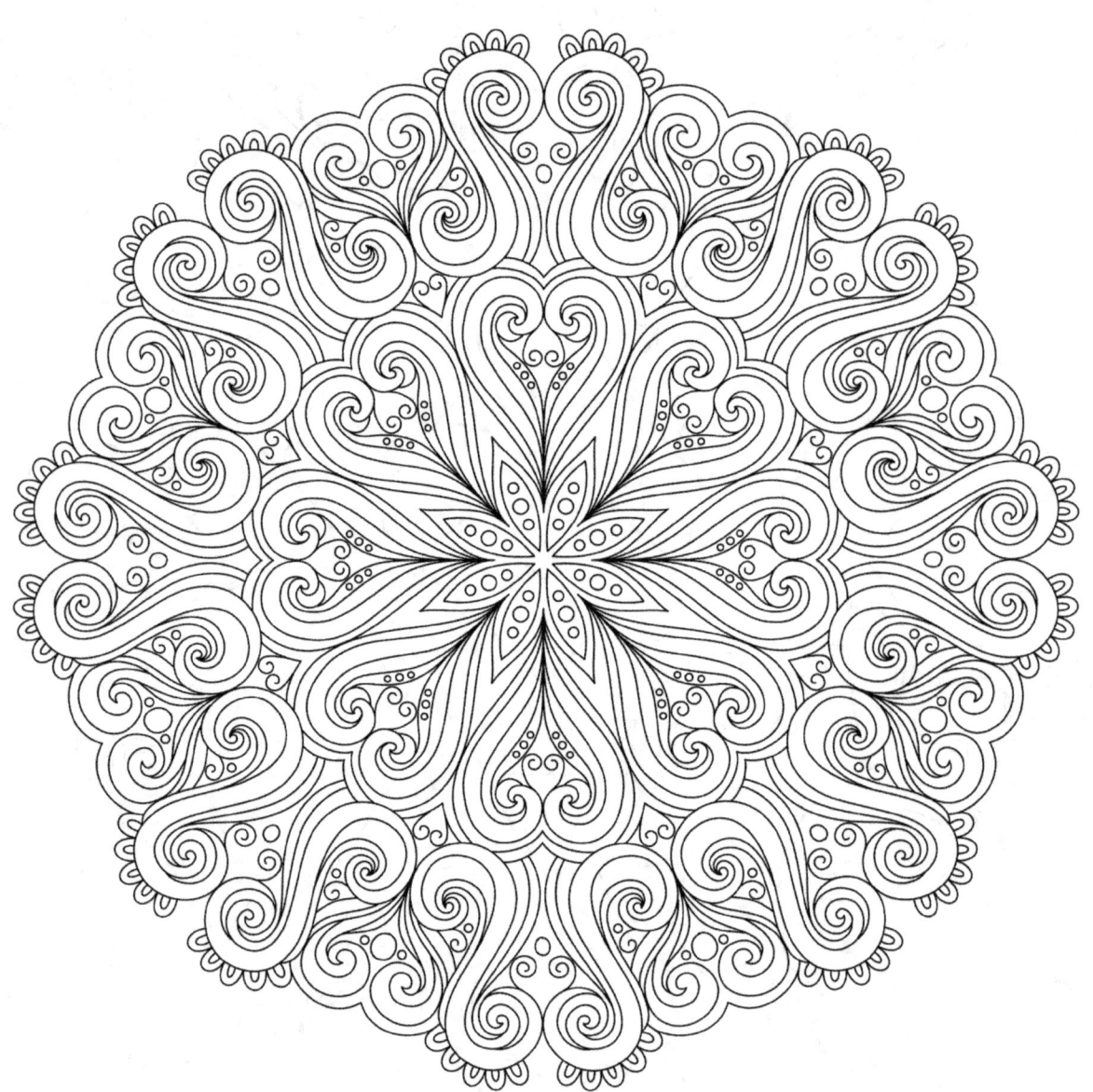

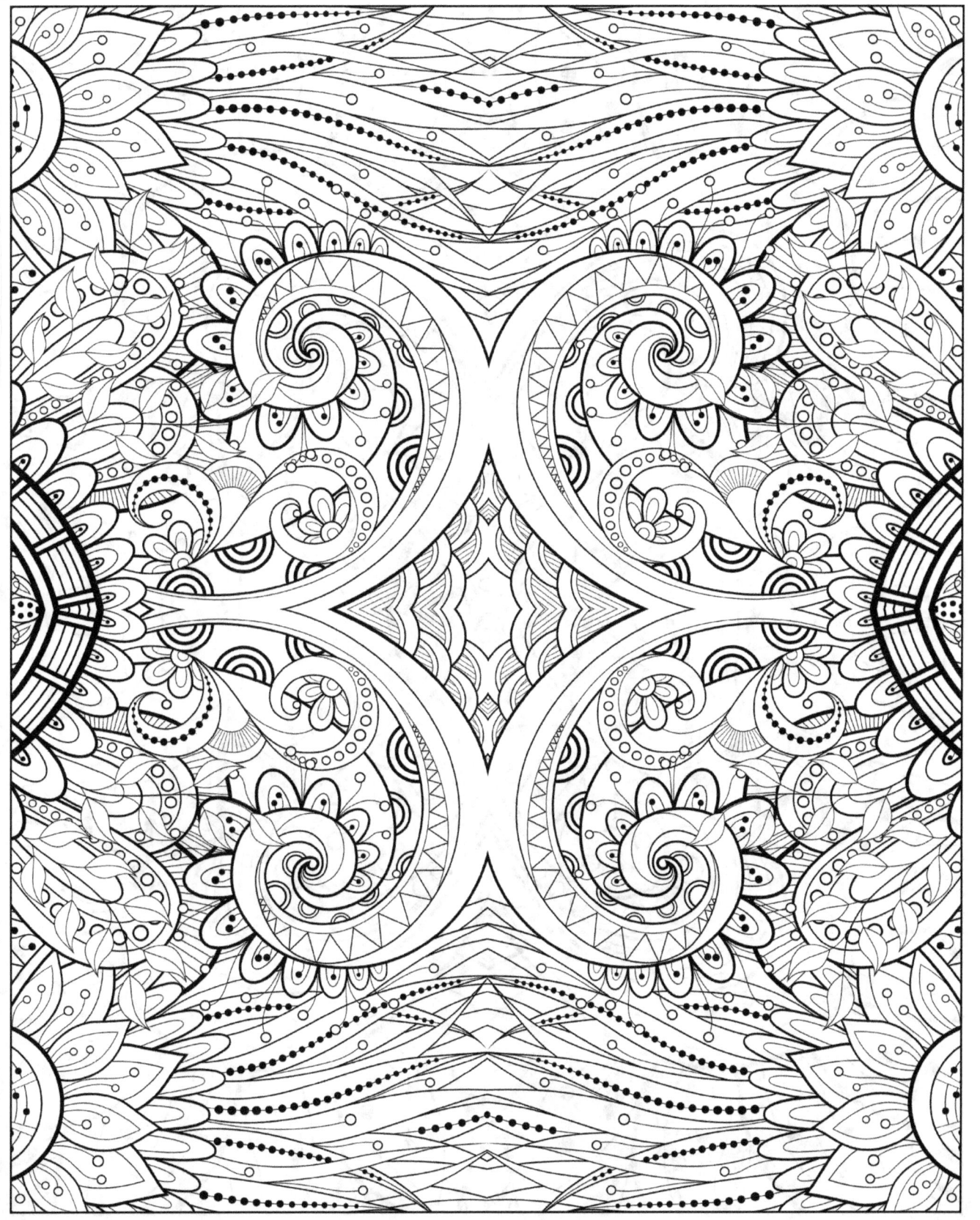

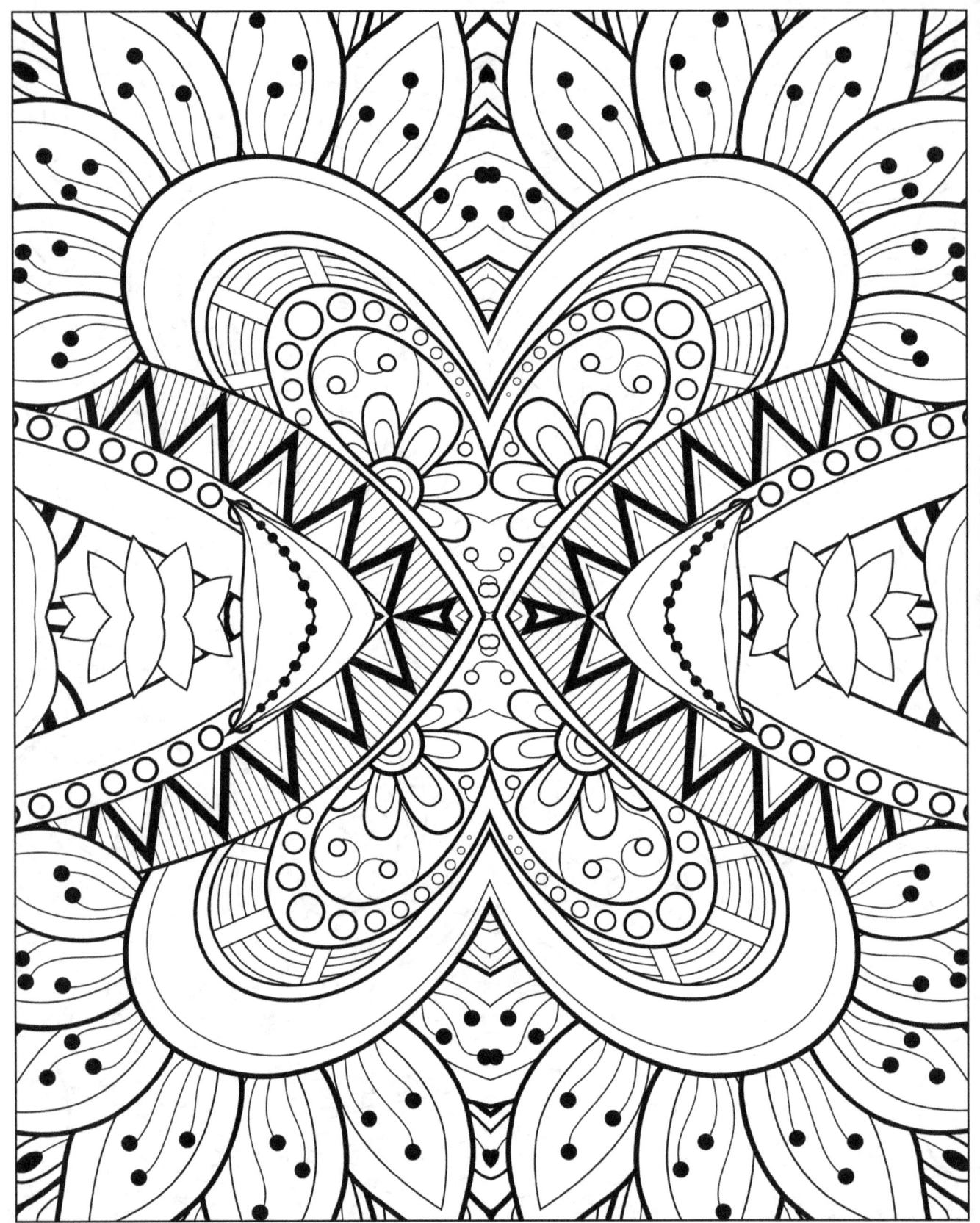

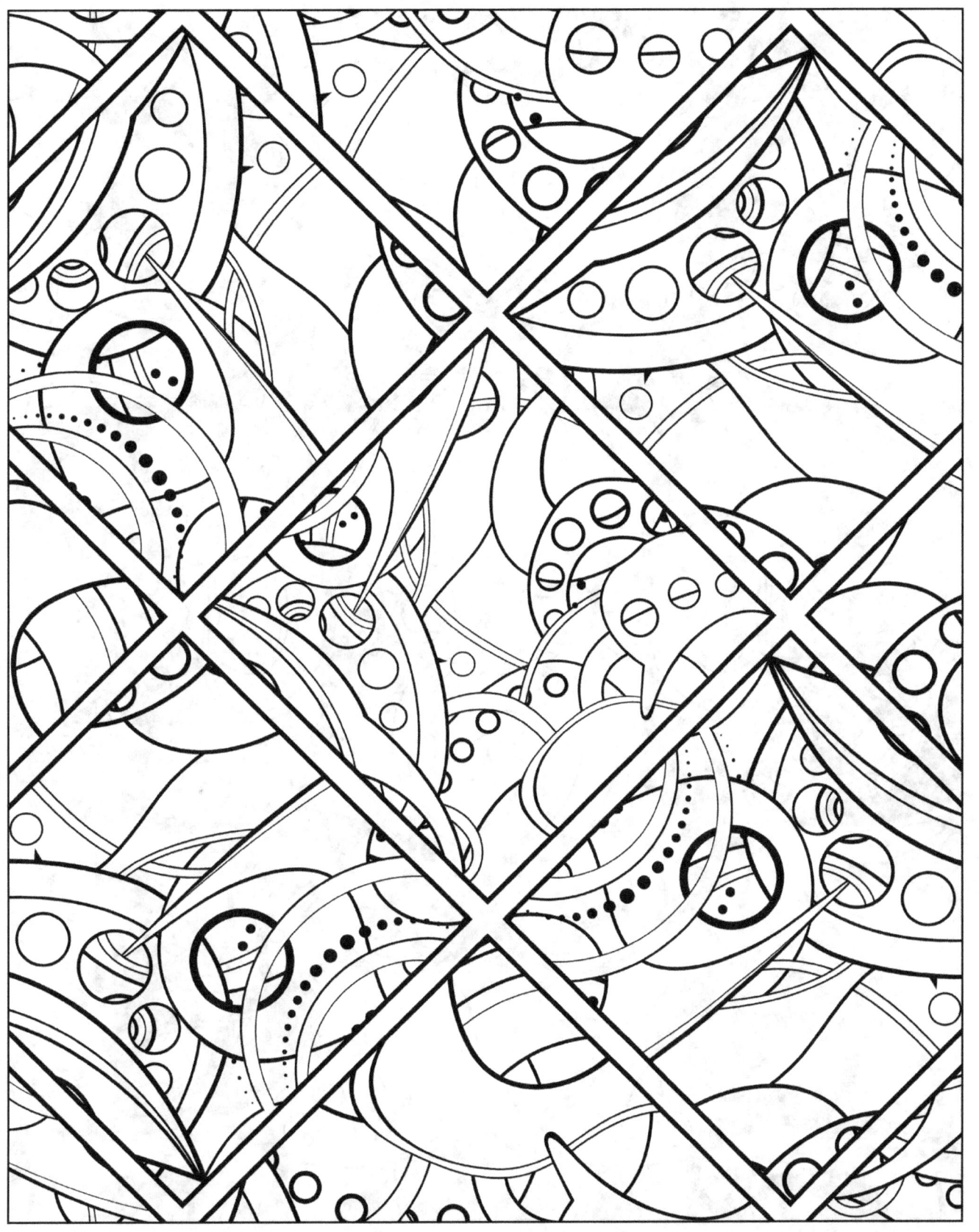

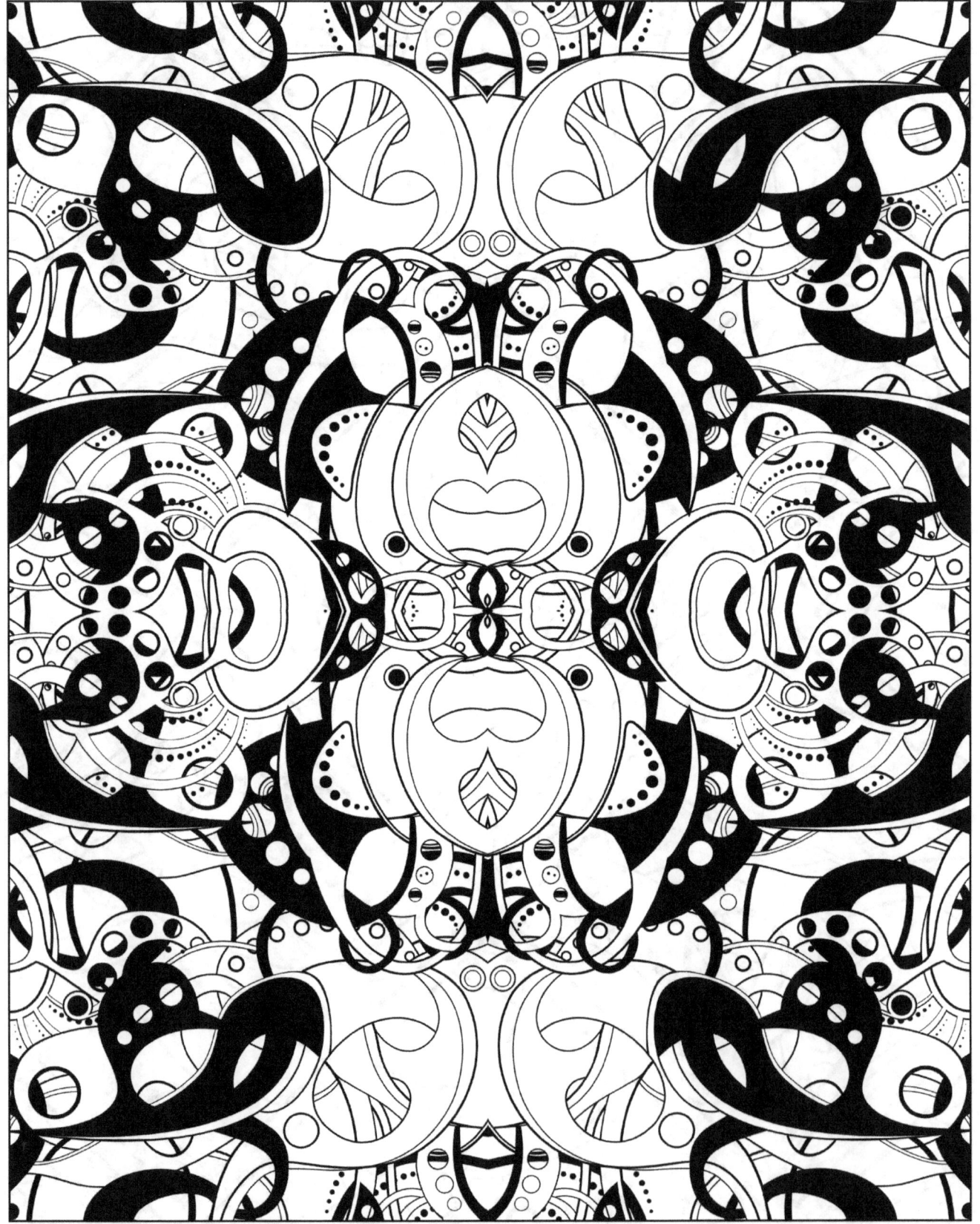

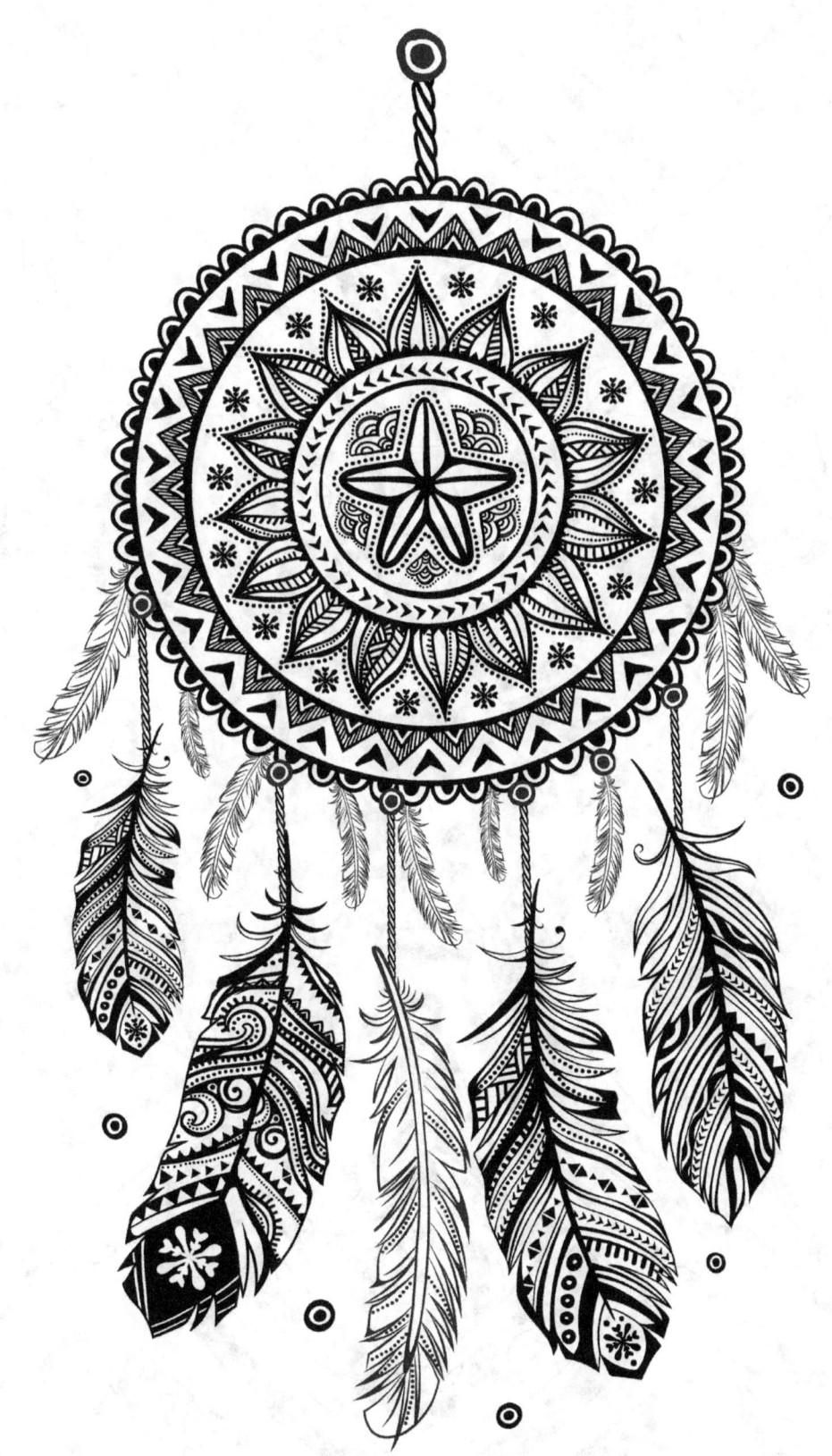

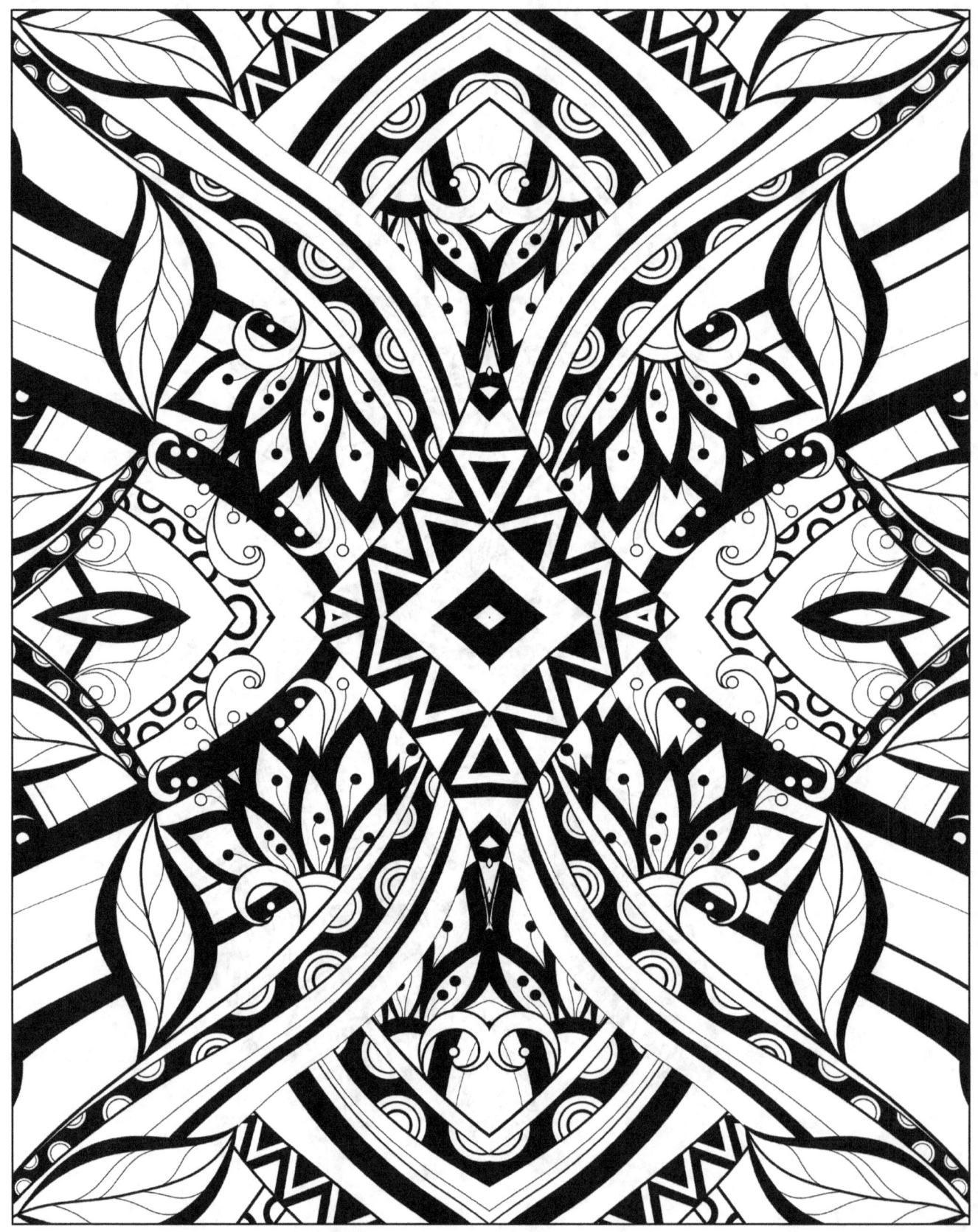

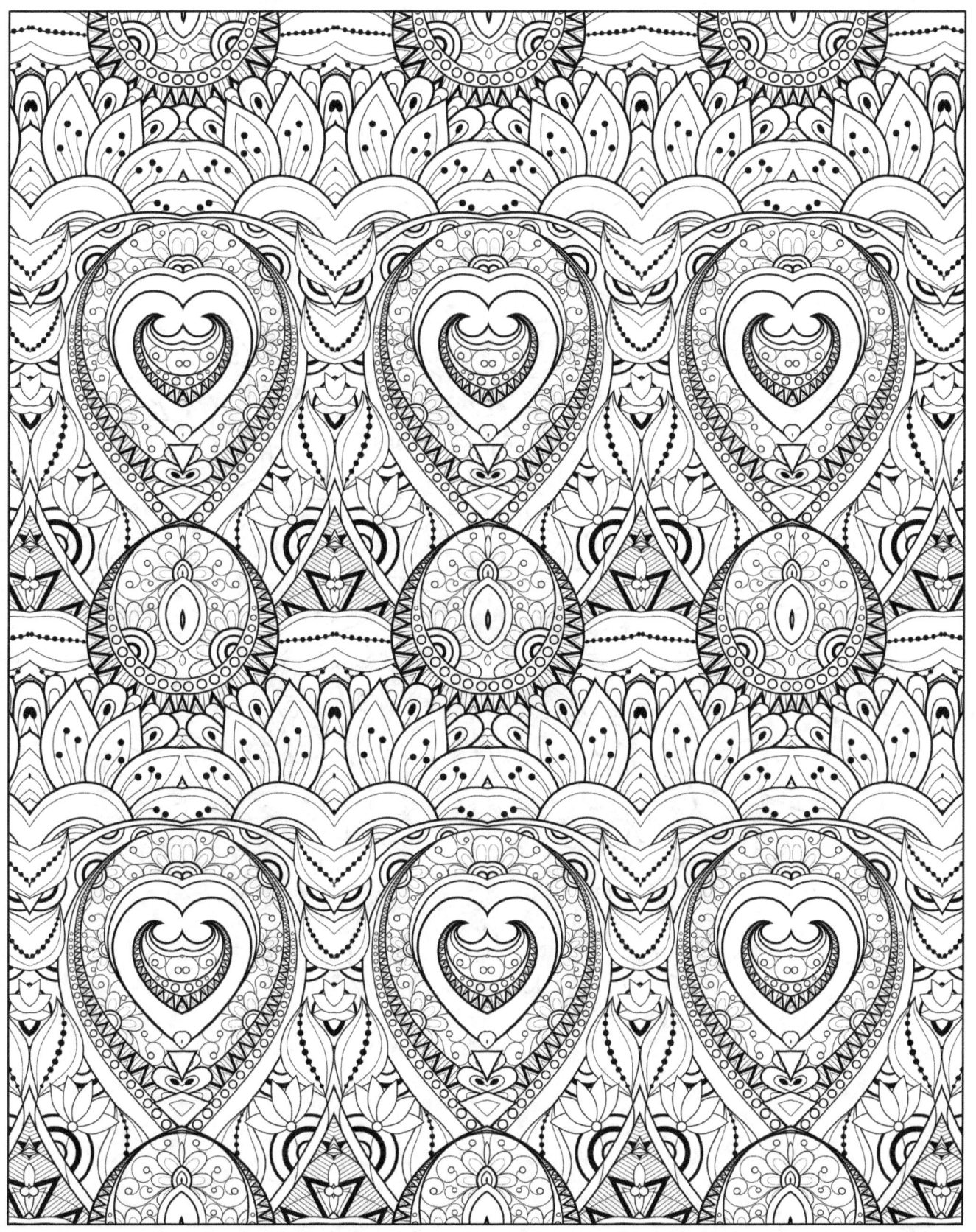

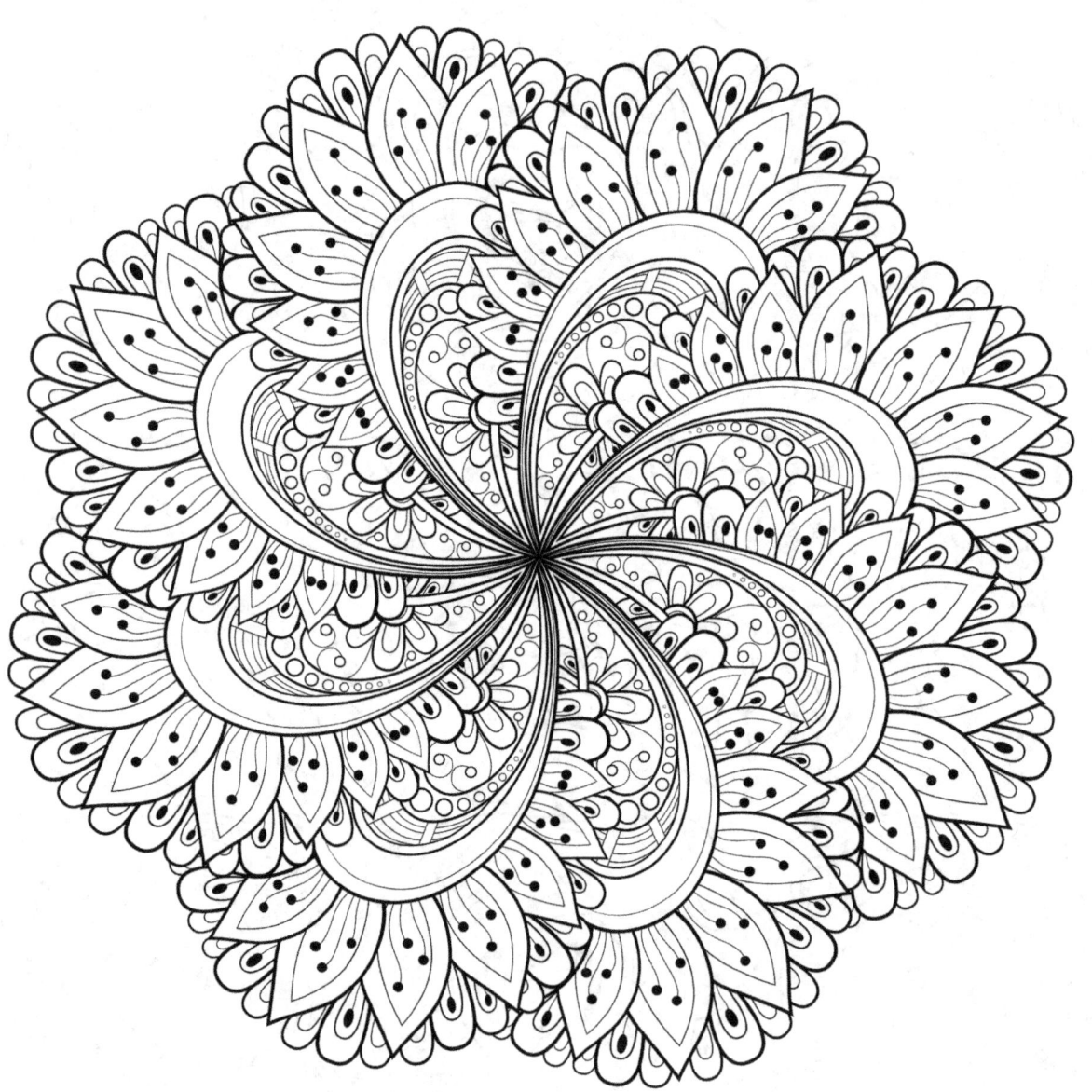

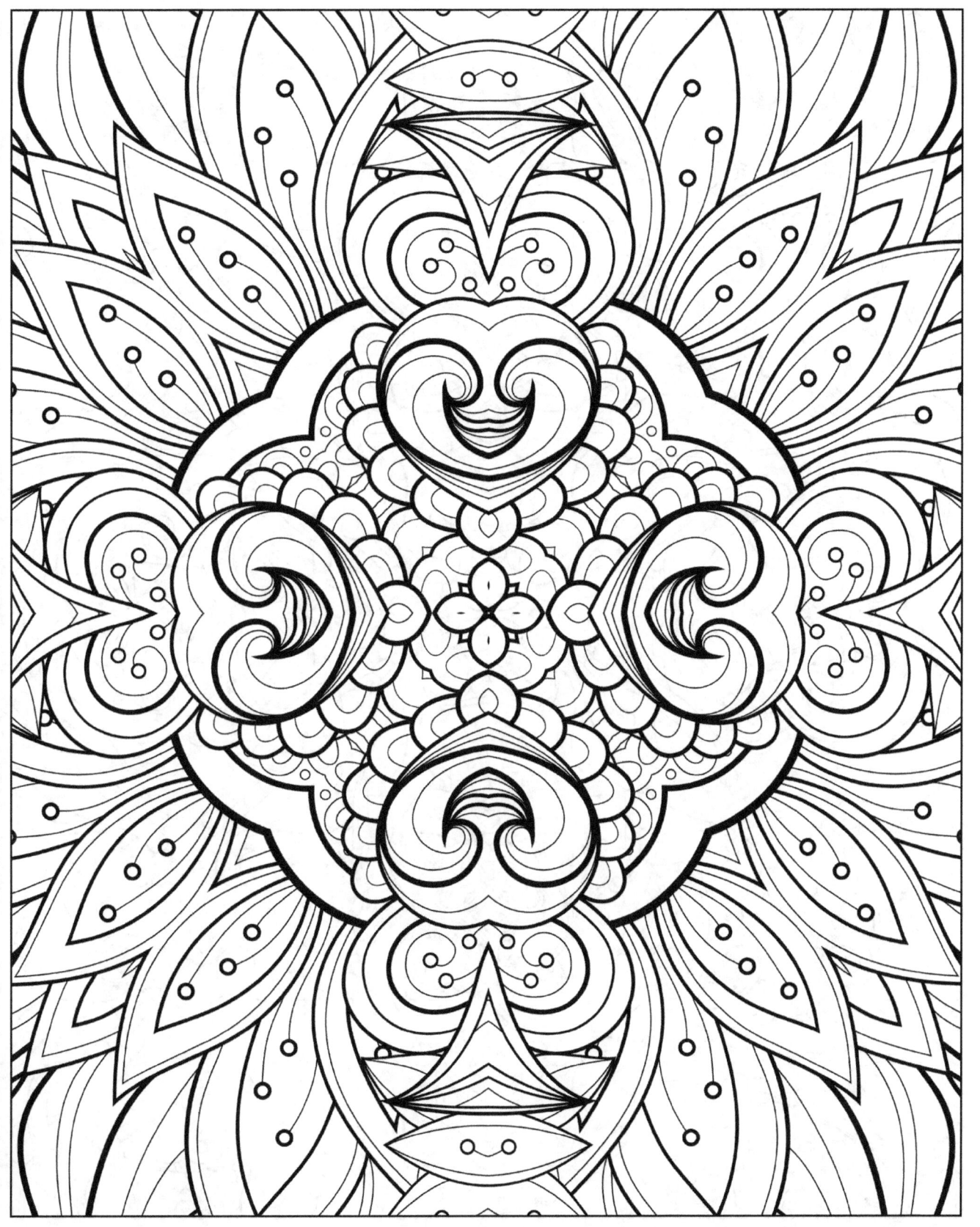

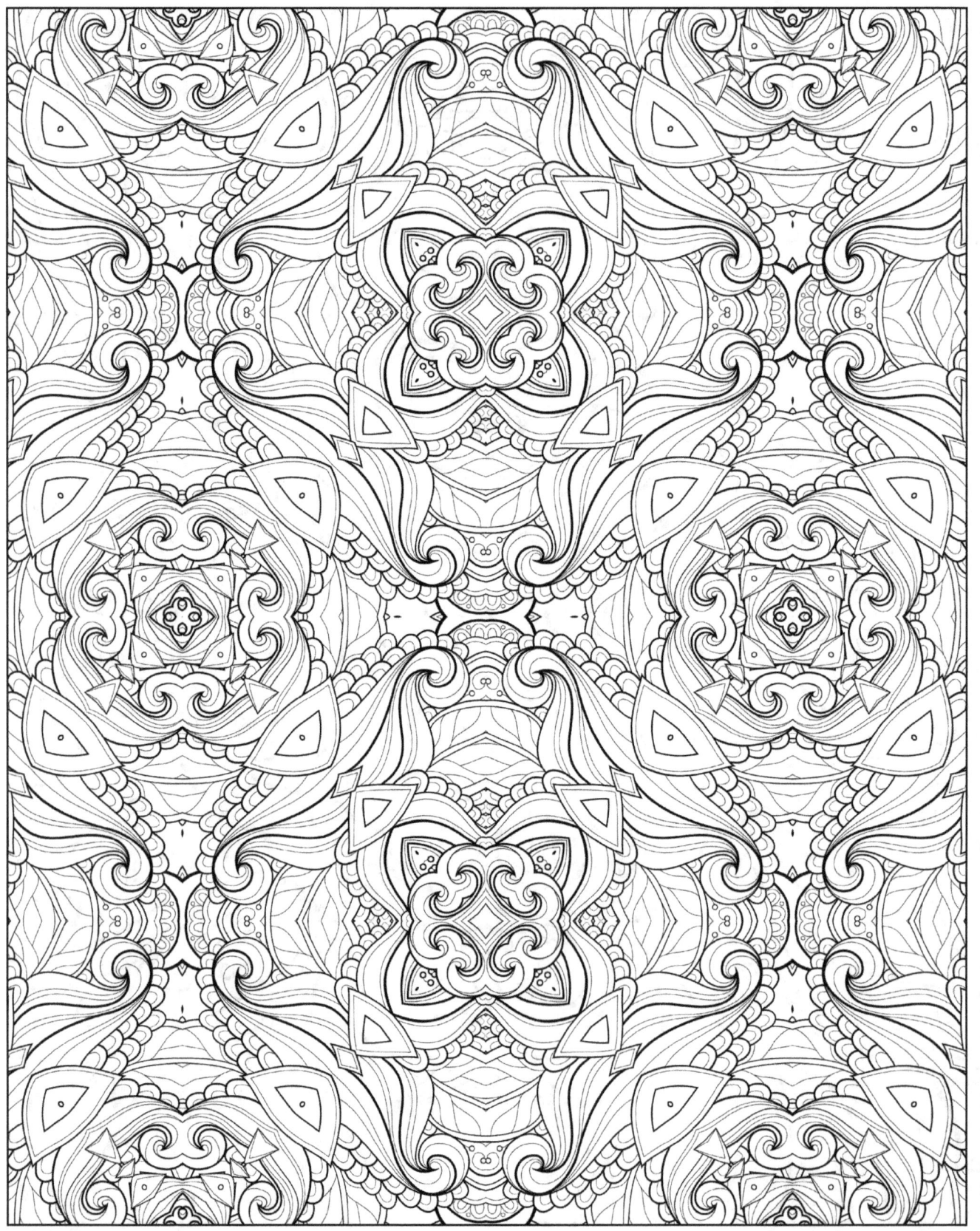

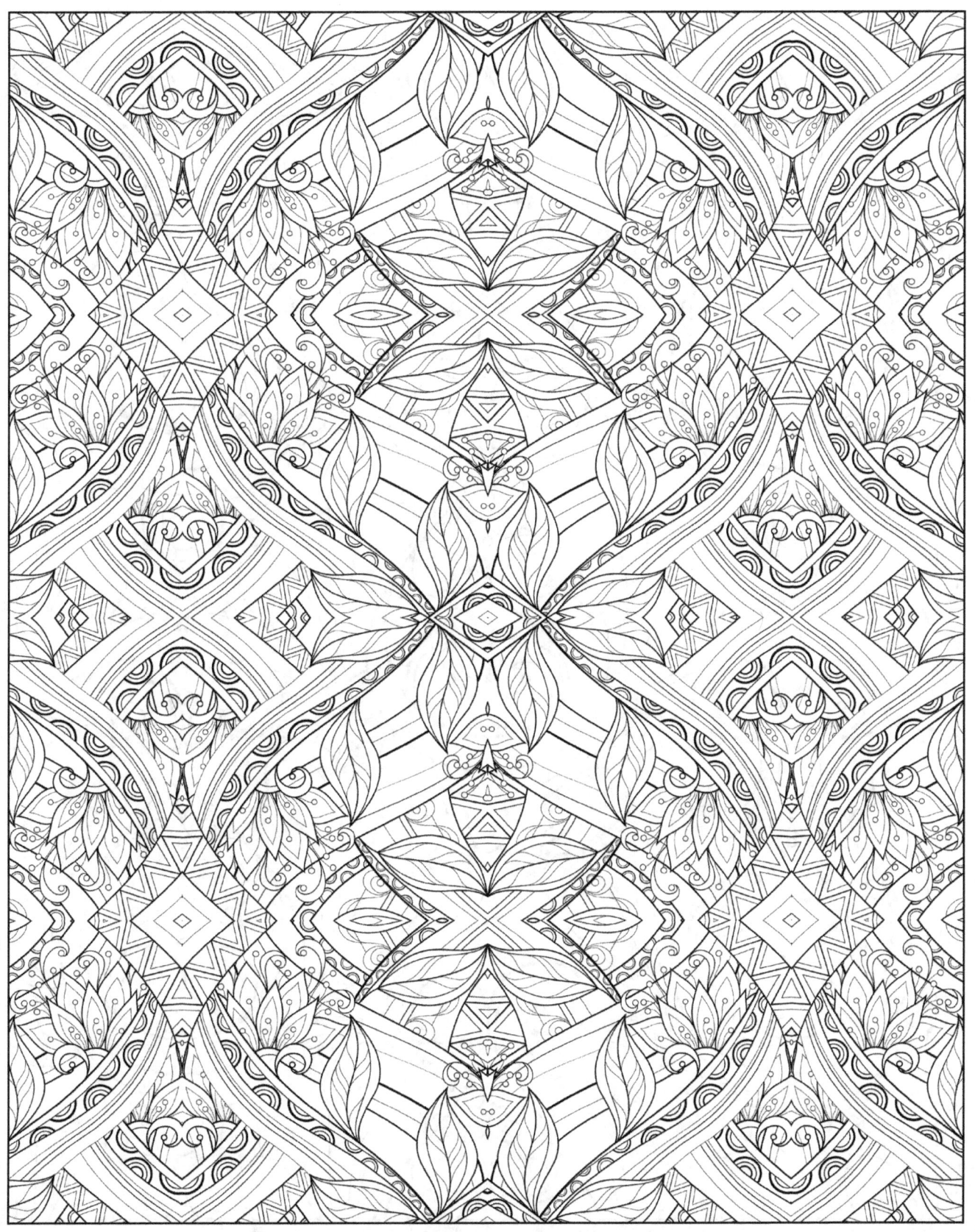

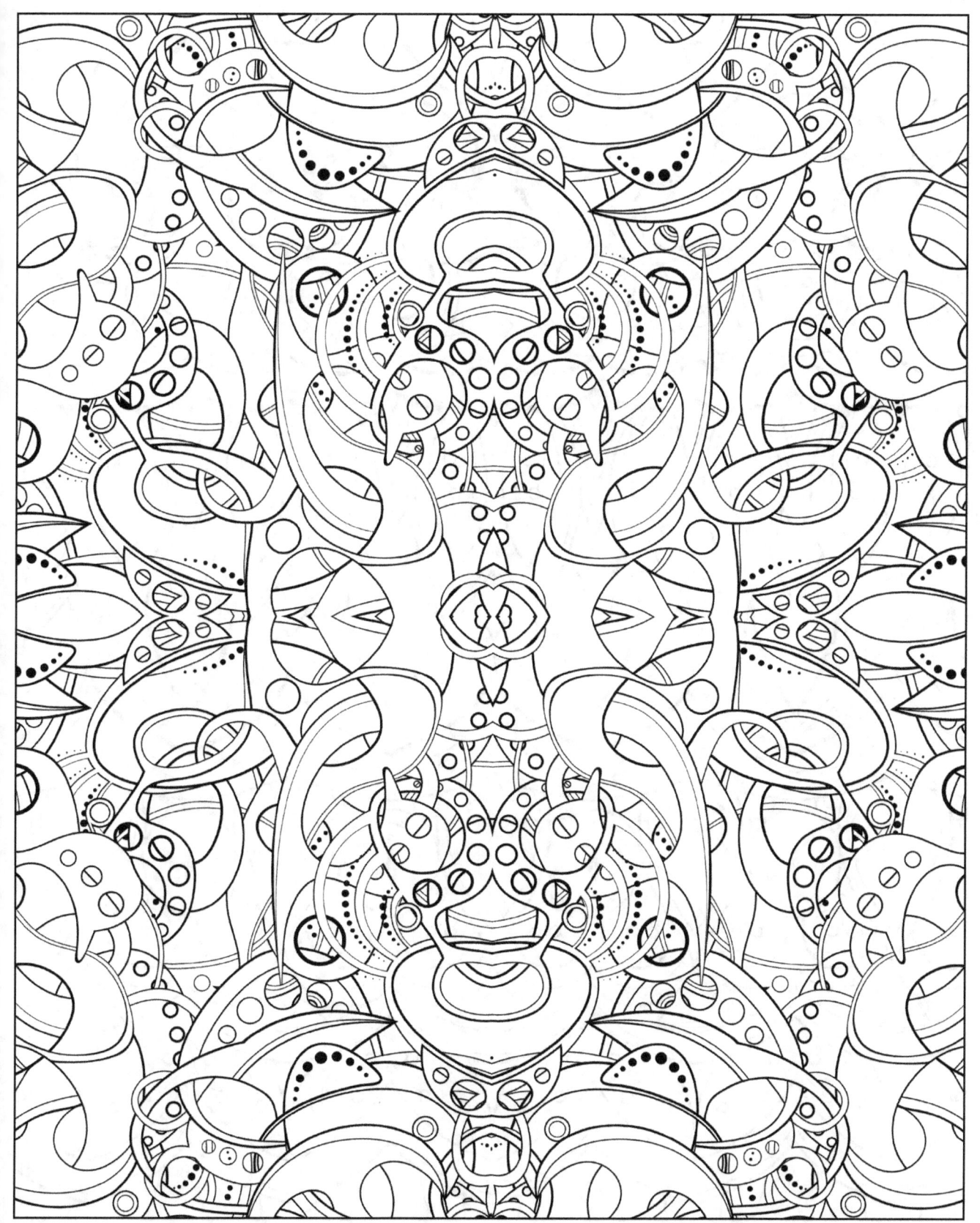

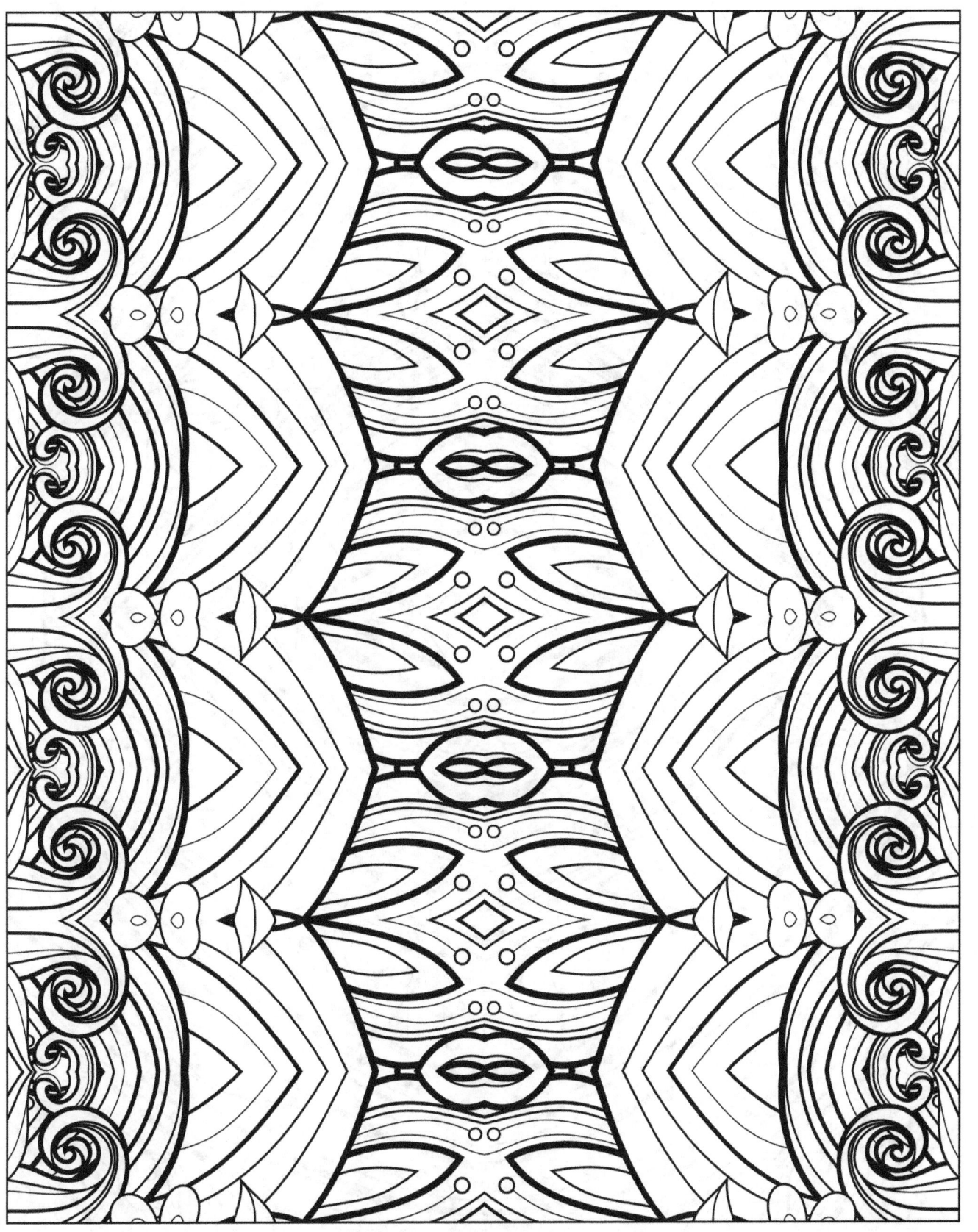

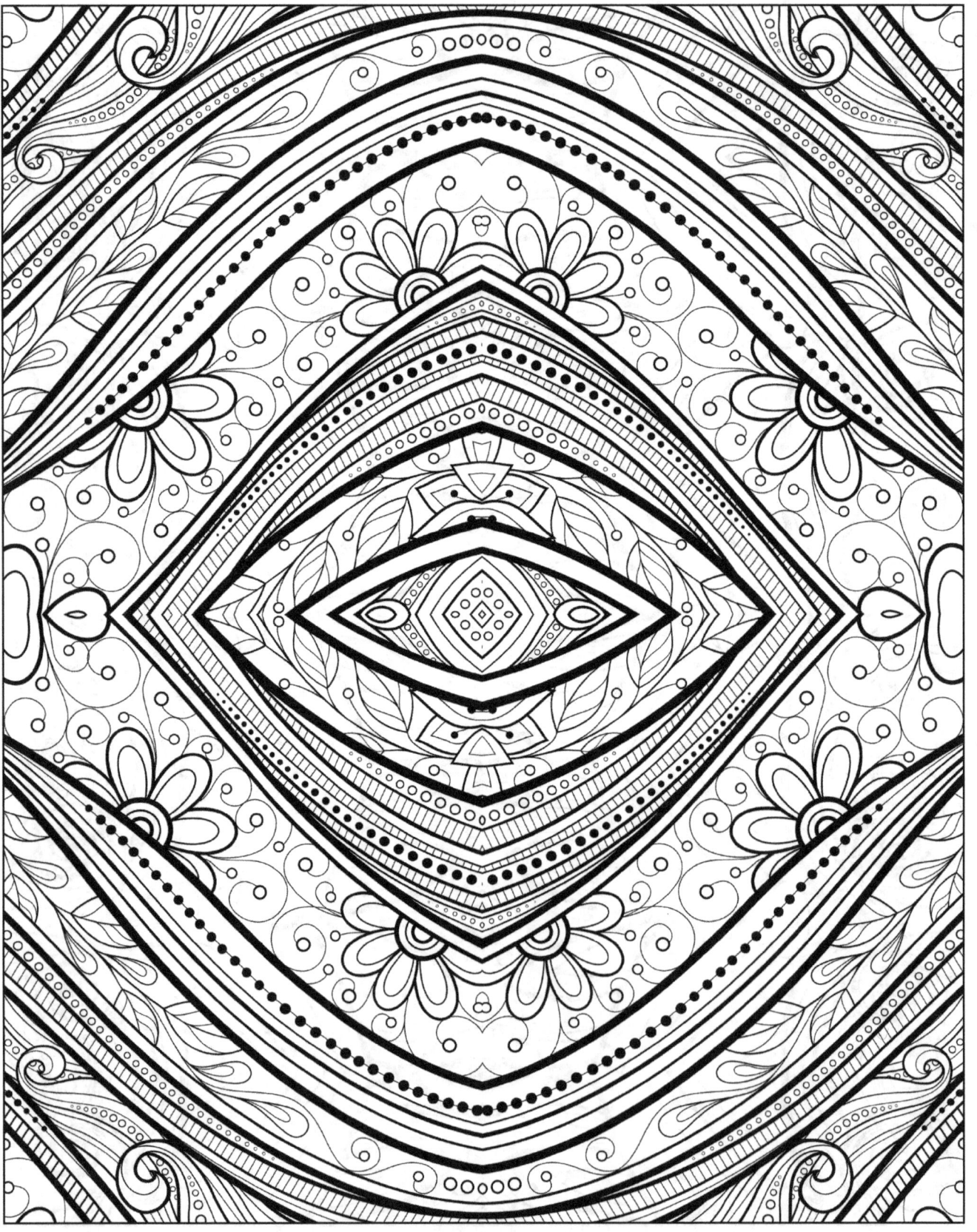

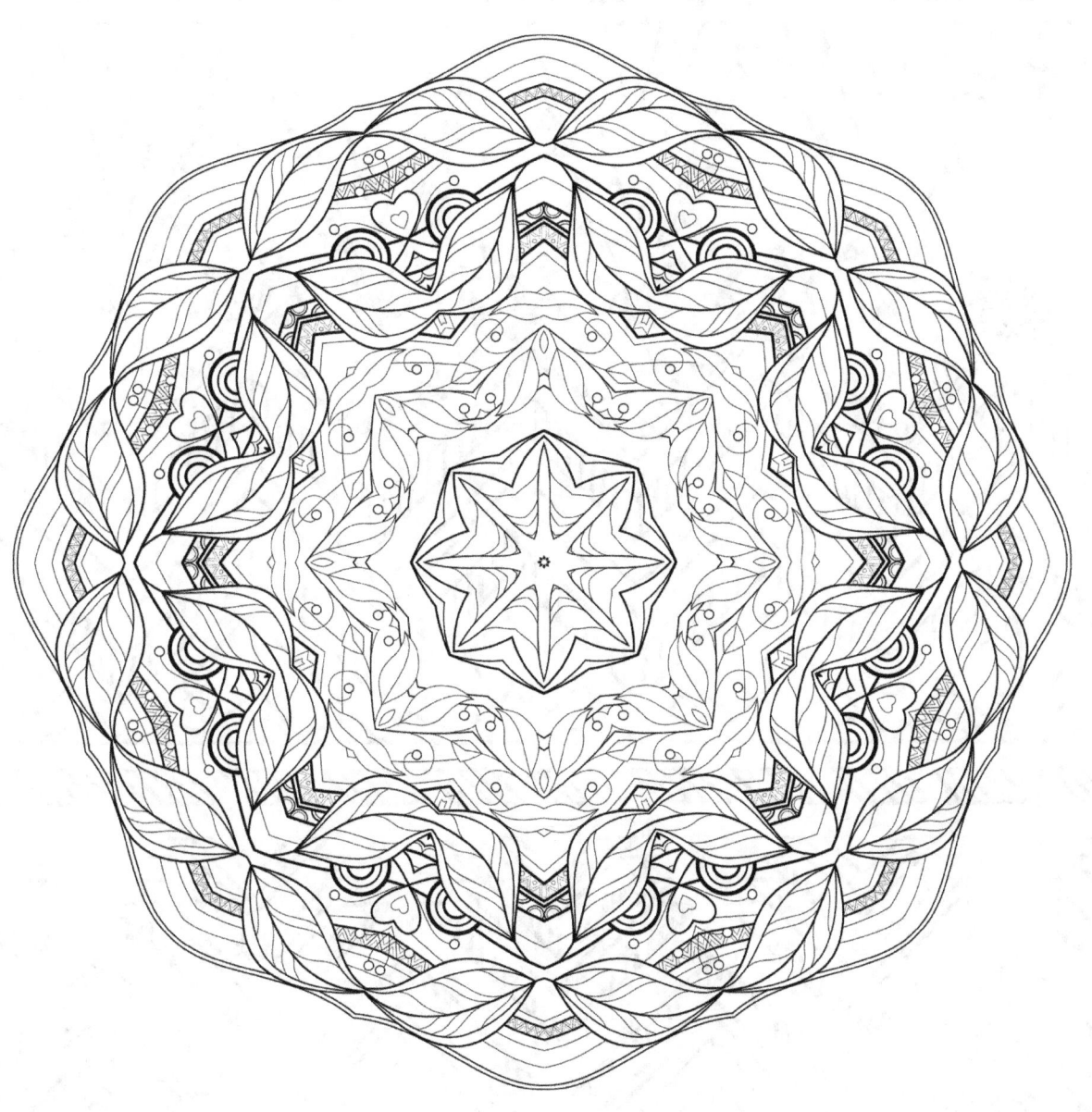

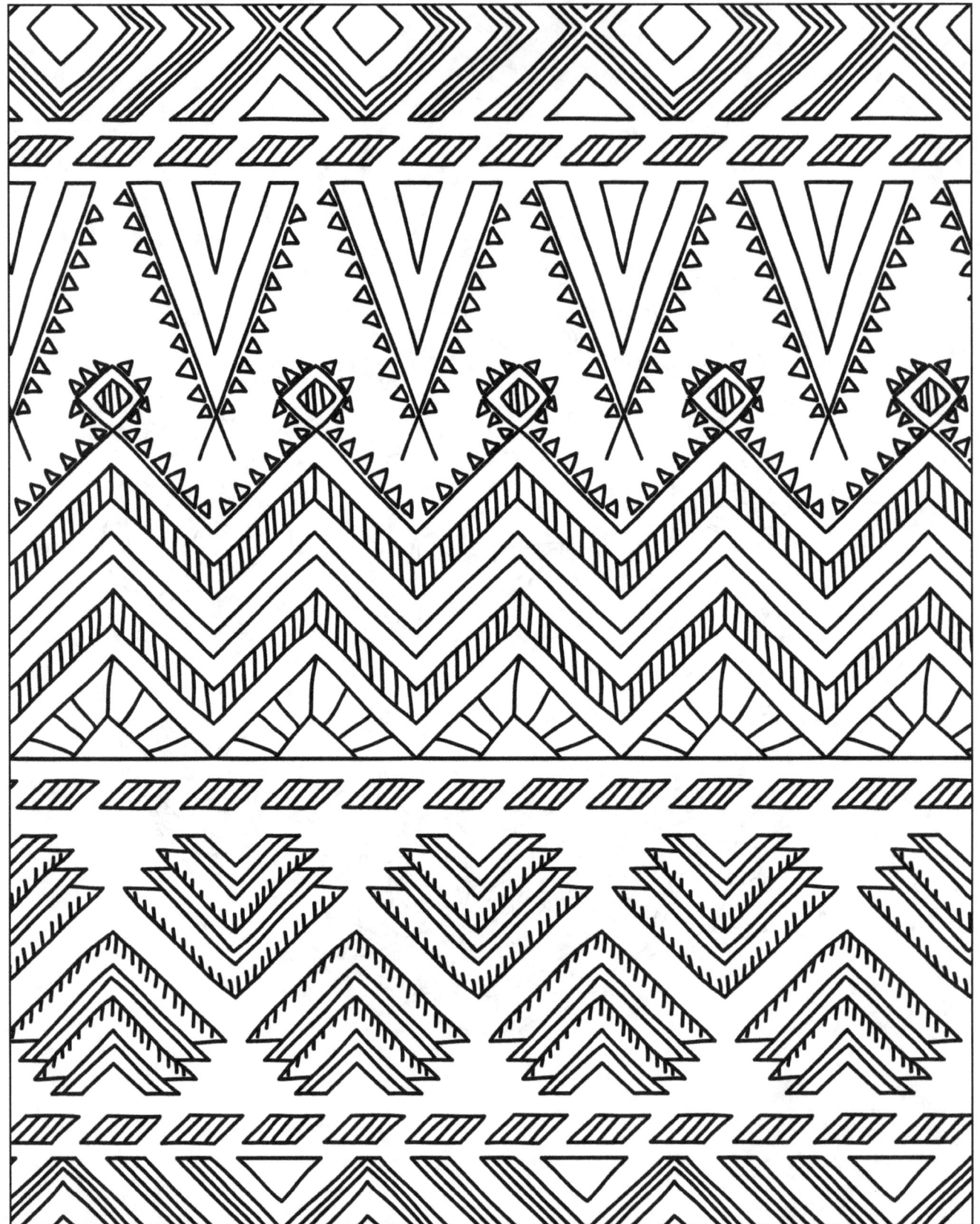

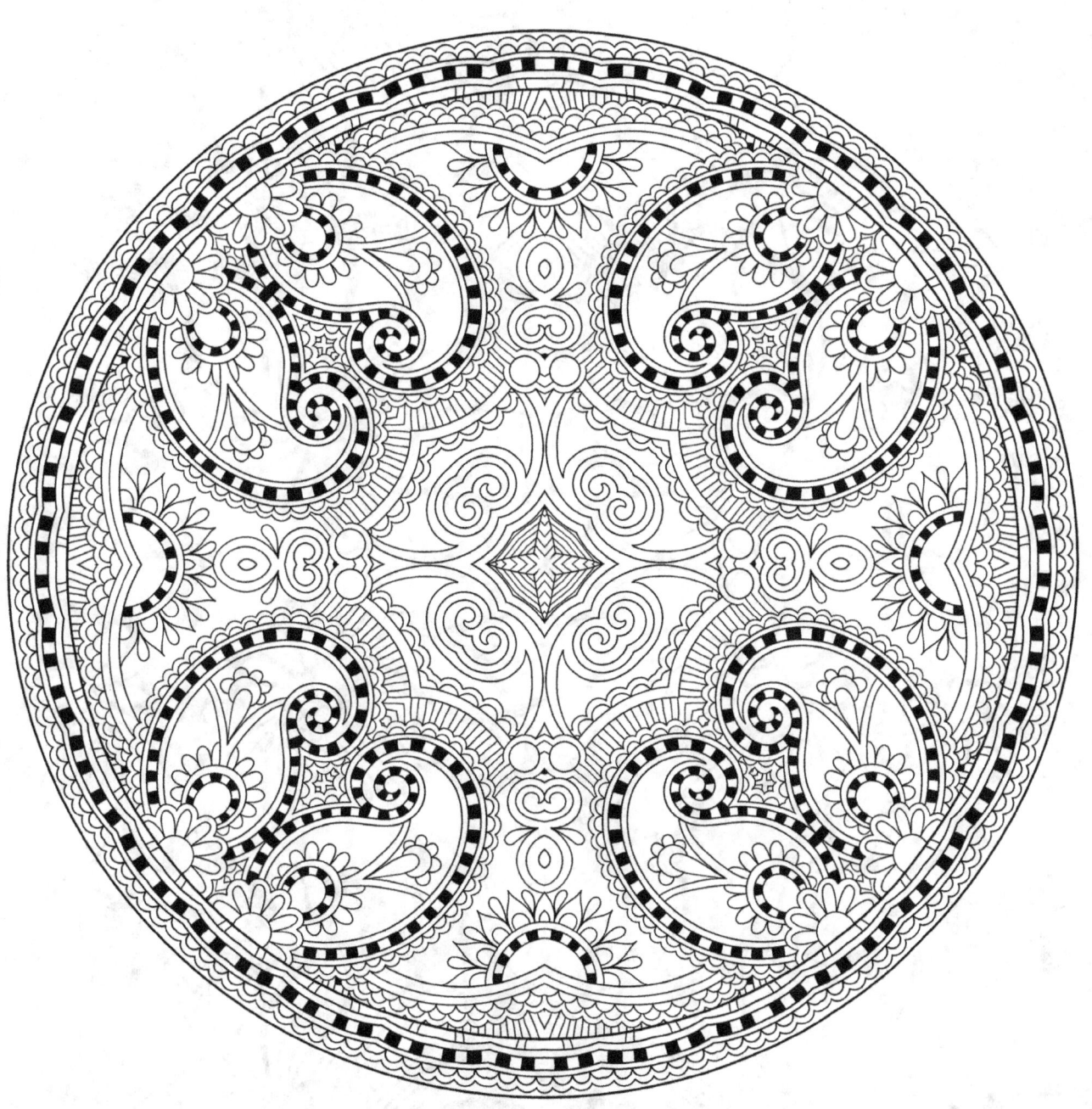

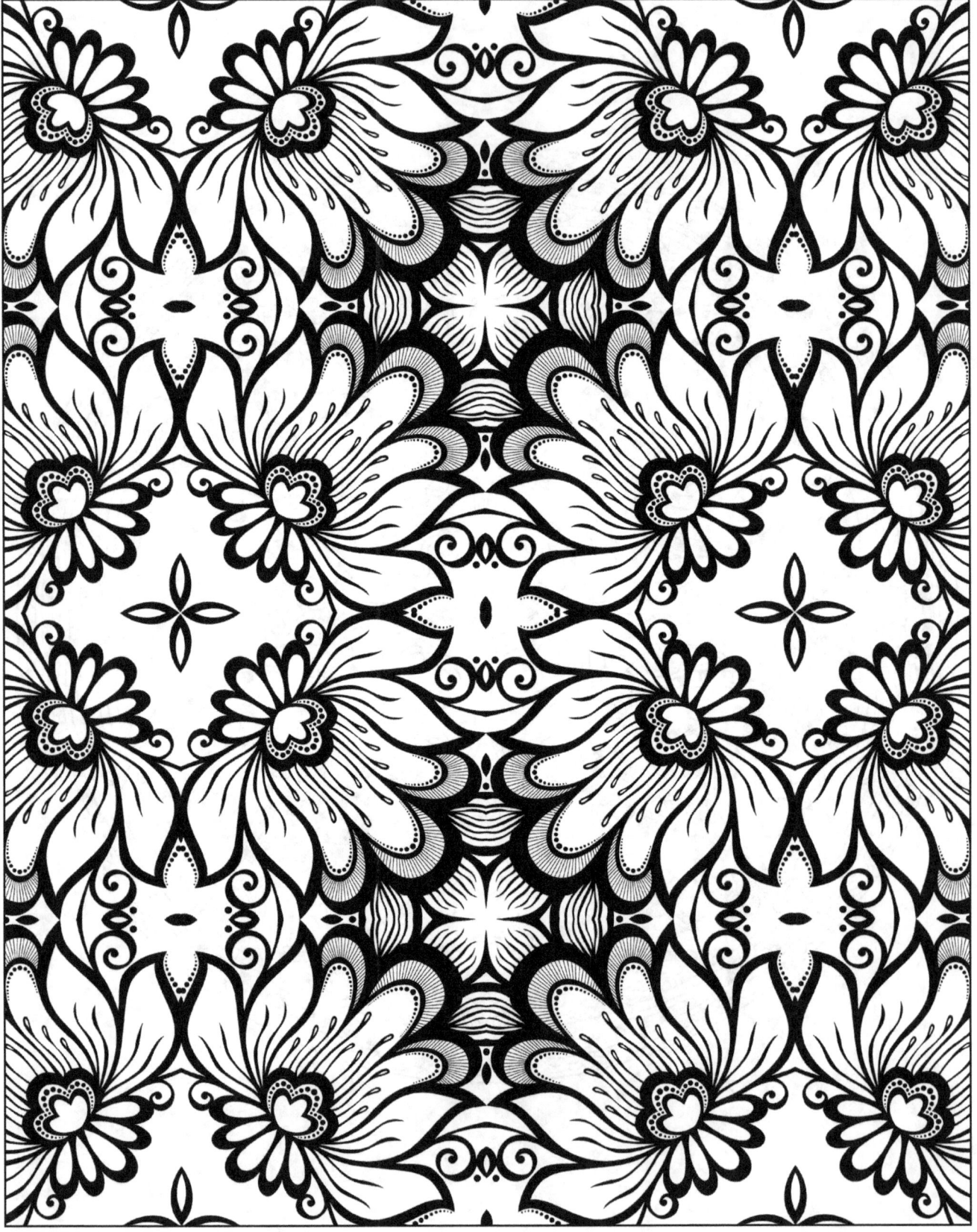

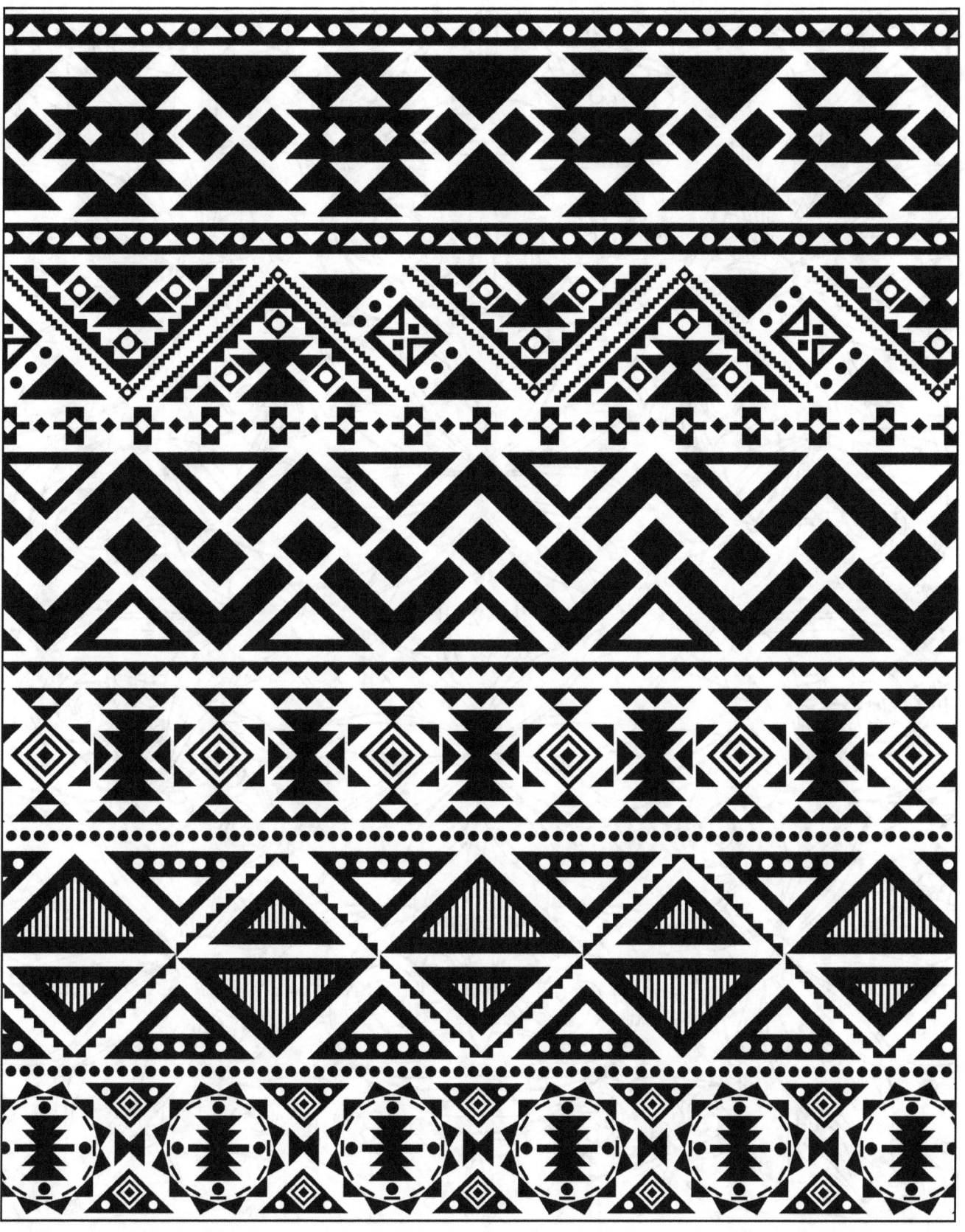

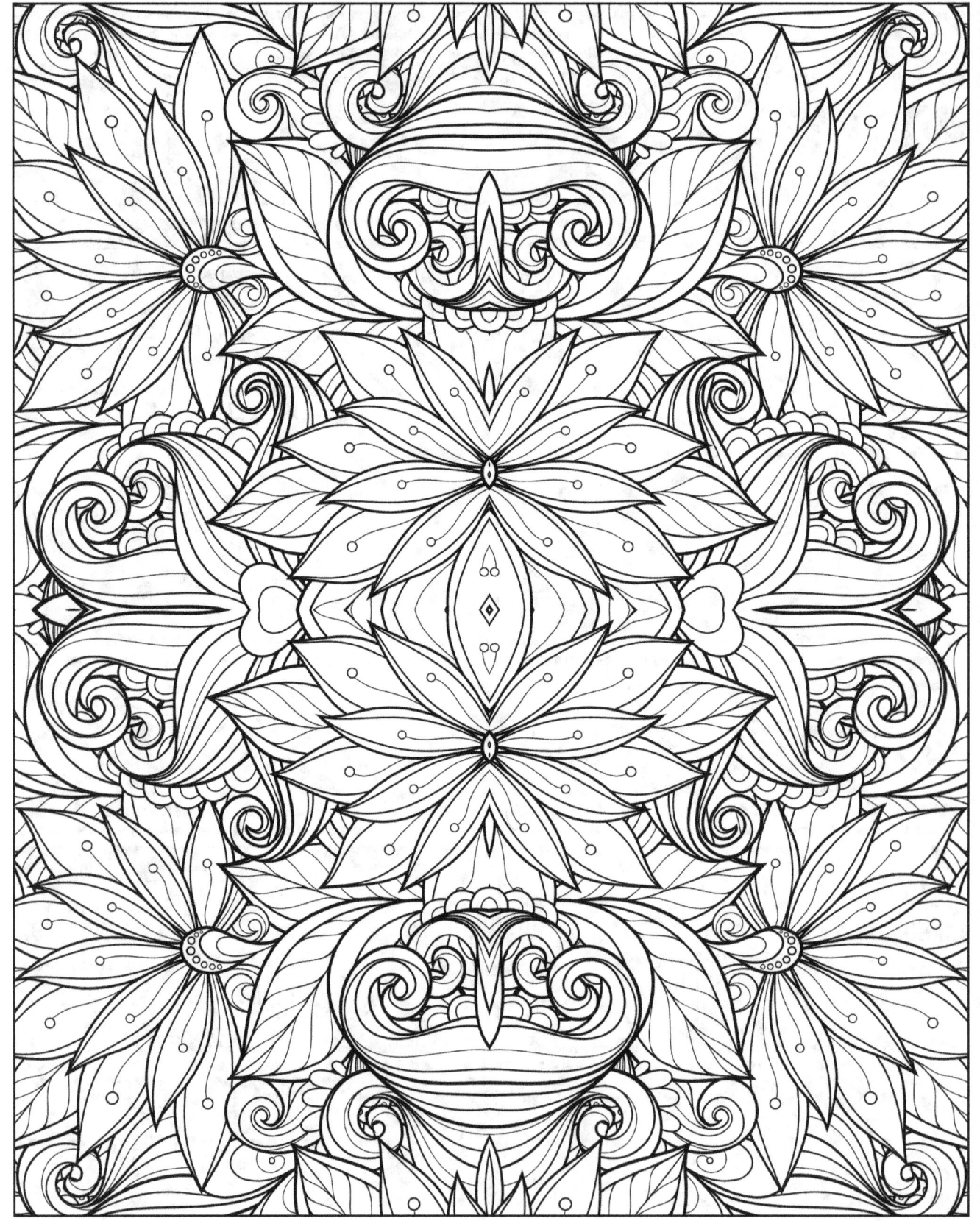

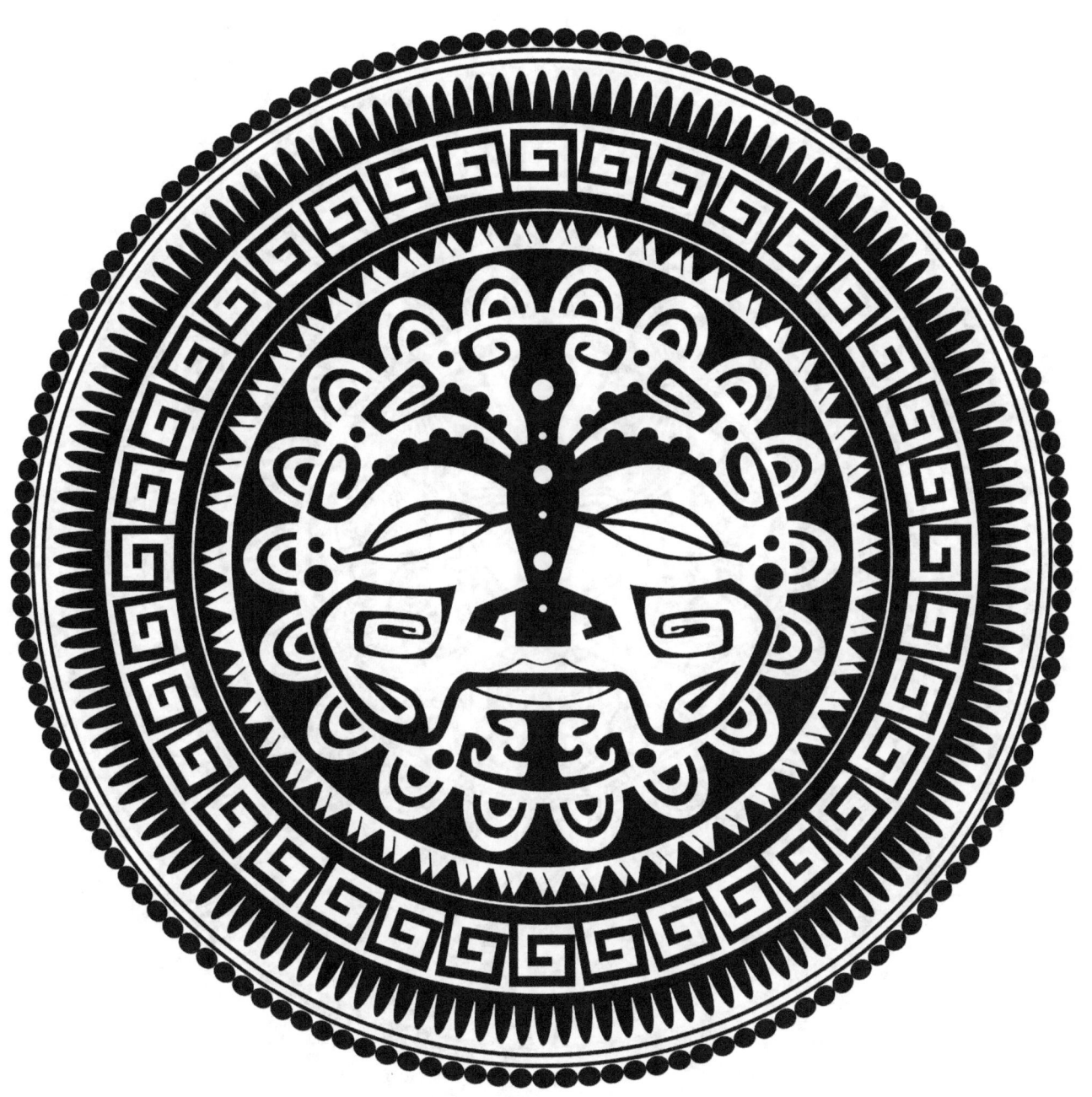

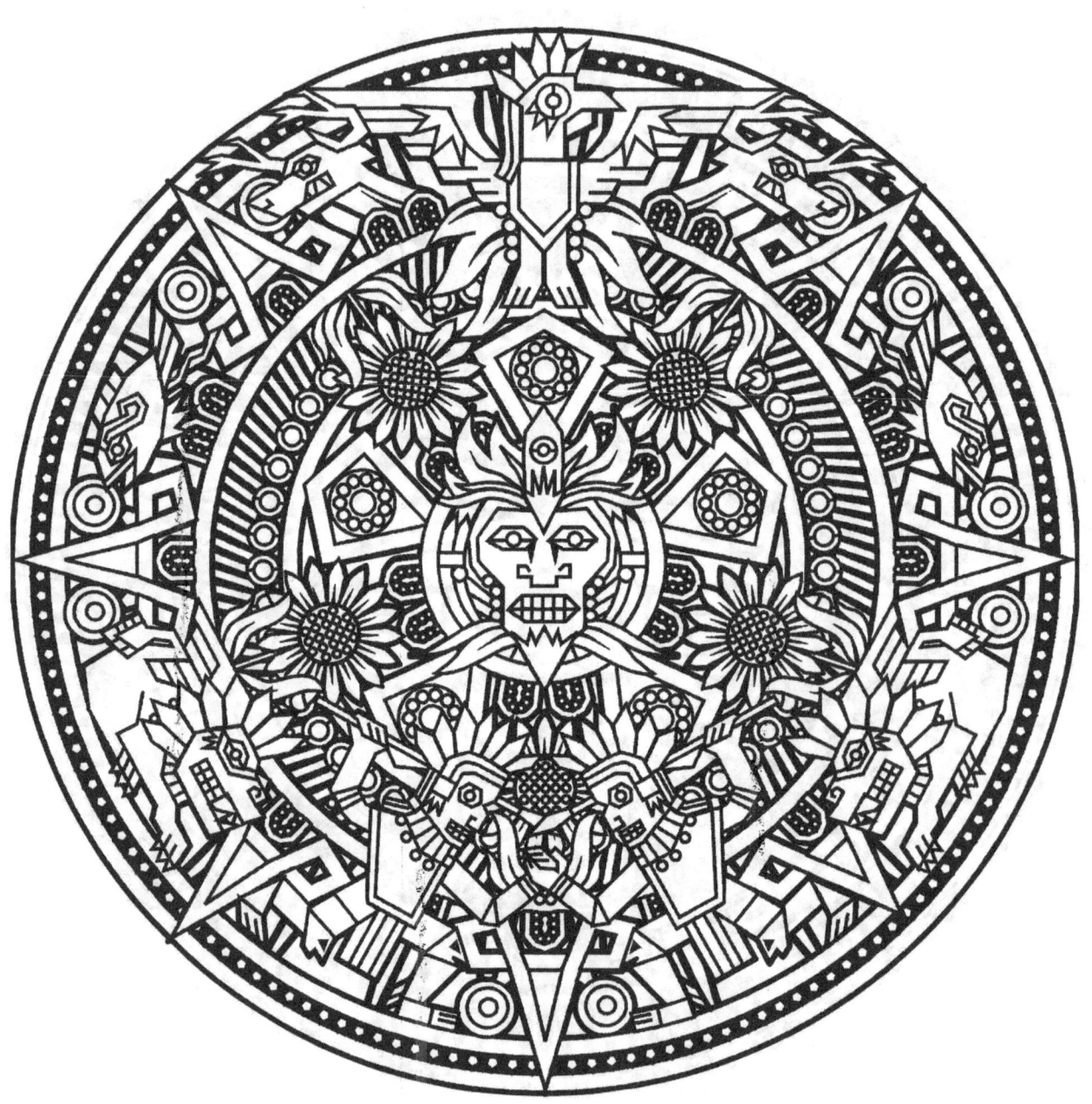

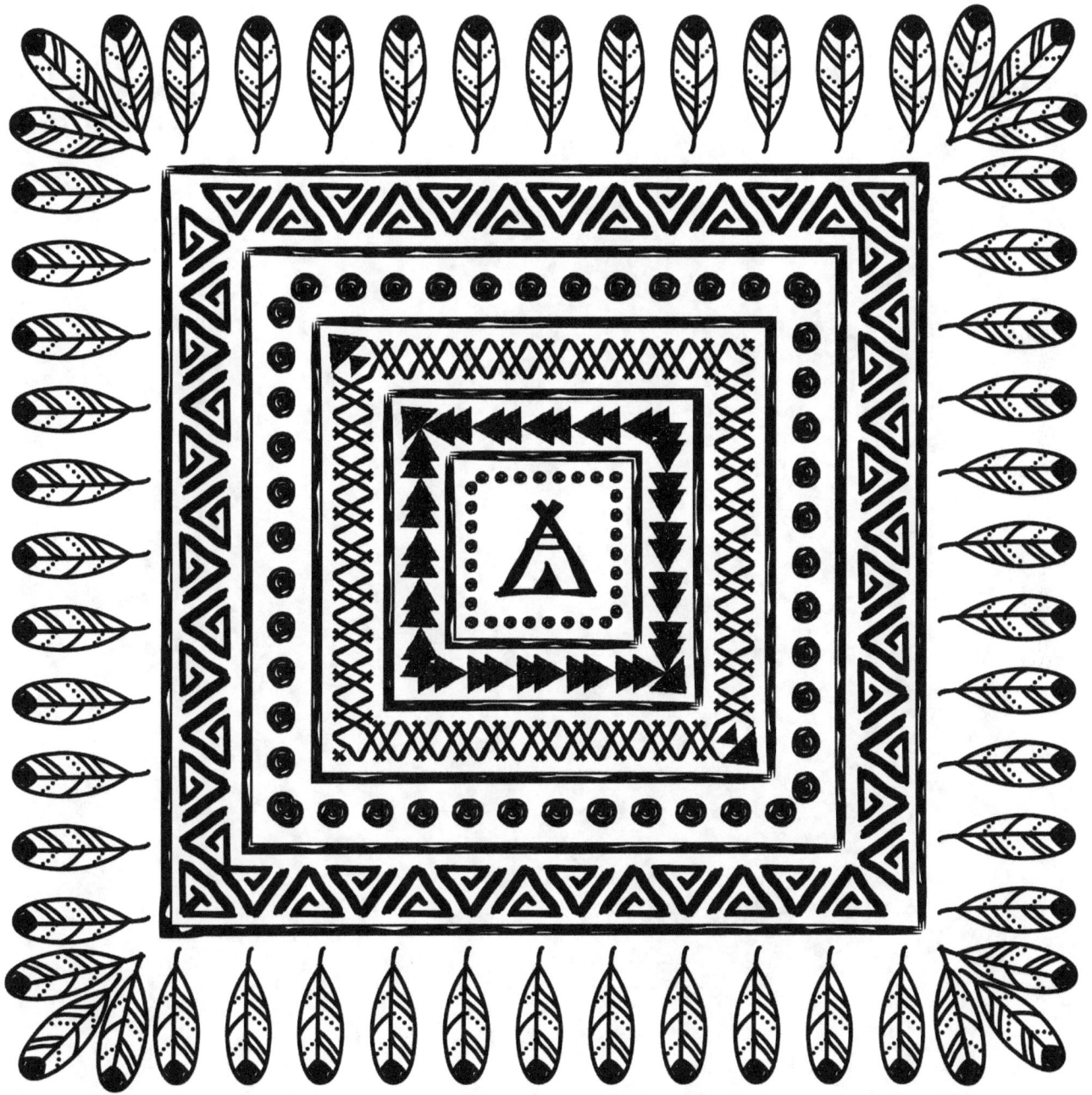